Manual for the

STEAMPUNK

TAROT

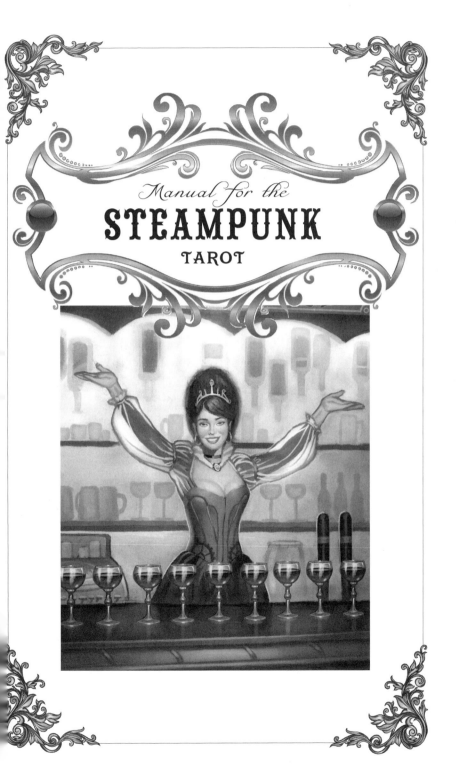

BARBARA MOORE

arot has been a part of Barbara Moore's personal and professional lives for over two decades. In college, tarot intrigued her with its marvelous blending of mythology, psychology, art, and history. Today she continues her tarot journey, both by learning from others and sharing her ideas through writing and teaching. Indeed, this erstwhile Hermit is discovering that she is enjoying traveling all over the world to share her love of tarot. Barbara enjoys writing about tarot; some of her favorite works include *A Guide to Mystic Faerie Tarot*, *The Gilded Tarot Companion*, *Tarot for Beginners*, and *Tarot Spreads: Layouts & Techniques to Empower Your Readings*.

ALY FELL

*P*rior to illustrating, UK-based Aly was an animator on TV shows such as *Dangermouse* and *Count Duckula*, eventually working for a spell in computer games. He now illustrates, particularly enjoying creating strong female characters, and his work has been published in *Spectrum*, *Exotique*, and *Expose*. He is also the coeditor of two fantasy art collections, and his art has been featured on the cover of magazines such as *ImagineFX*. He and his wife like to travel to as many places as they can and enjoy the dark side of culture, being fairly active on the Goth scene.

Manual for the
STEAMPUNK
TAROT

BARBARA MOORE

ILLUSTRATED BY ALY FELL

Llewellyn Publications
WOODBURY, MINNESOTA

FIRST EDITION
Second Printing, 2012

Author photo by Lisa Novak; illustrator photo by Aly Fell
Book design by Rebecca Zins
Cover and interior credits: abstract wallpaper (iStockphoto.com/Luseen),
gold and black designs (iStockphoto.com/S-E-R-G-O),
ornate background (iStockphoto.com/Oleksandr Bondarenko),
gold scroll frame (iStockphoto.com/Electric_Crayon)
Cover design by Kevin R. Brown
Illustrations © 2012 by Aly Fell

Llewellyn is a registered trademark of Llewellyn Worldwide Ltd.

ISBN 978-0-7387-2638-0
The Steampunk Tarot kit consists of a boxed set of
78 full-color cards and this perfect-bound book.

Llewellyn Publications
A Division of Llewellyn Worldwide Ltd.
2143 Wooddale Drive
Woodbury, MN 55125-2989
www.llewellyn.com

Printed in the United States of America

To Andrew. What a brilliant idea!
~Barbara

To Rosie, for being there.
~Aly

CONTENTS
table of

INTRODUCTION

Welcome to the Steampunk Tarot.

Nearly twenty years ago, during my role-playing game days, I discovered the concept of steampunk (does anyone remember Castle Falkenstein?), although I don't think most of us regular folk called it that; literary types most certainly did, though. For anyone who loves sci-fi, from *Star Trek* to *Firefly* to *Doctor Who* and anything in Victorian period clothing, steampunk is a very happy world indeed.

Sometime in 2005, during a discussion about man and machine, the past and the future, nature and technology, and, of course, fashion, a colleague suggested that I make a steampunk-themed tarot. Knowing it was a very niche subgenre, I filed the idea away, thinking I had plenty of time before developing the idea and presenting it to my publisher.

Shortly thereafter, in 2006, I started collecting links to websites and portfolios of artists who might be a good match for the deck.

And then, in 2009, a great publisher of fantasy and science fiction, Tor, proclaimed October to be Steampunk Month. That's when I began writing the card descriptions that had been taking shape in my mind for nearly four years. They must have been ready to manifest because once I began, they flowed almost effortlessly, as if channeled from somewhere other than myself—as if from another time and place that never was.

In January 2010, after two months of intense searching for an artist, I found Aly Fell's website…in particular, his image called *Judith* (which later was modified and is now our Queen of Cups). I knew the moment I saw that picture that I wanted Aly on this project. What did I do? I wrote a long email to a perfect stranger, asking him if he would be interested in taking on the task of giving line, color, and composition to my words, bringing them to life. As luck would have it, he was interested. In addition, he did know a little something about tarot.

Since then, we've been plugging away, forgive the pun, full steam ahead. We are proud to present what we both consider some of our best work. May these cards and this book help you achieve your best work as you craft your life and chart your journey.

A BIT ABOUT STEAMPUNK

Once in a while, when discussing this project, people ask me what steampunk is. It is easy enough to Google the word; you'll find lots of interesting information. My favorite advice for a super-quick introduction is to tell people to use the "Google Images" function and search *steampunk* or *steampunk fashion*. Steampunk is certainly more than costumes, but the visual aesthetic conveys the sensibility very well.

As far as verbal descriptions of the concept, I have heard a few. Some of the more clever ones include:

What the past would look like if the future had happened sooner.

What happens when Goths discover the color brown.

Retro-tech.

Fashion and witty observations aside, it is true that steampunk is a genre—or more accurately, in my opinion, an aesthetic—that has its roots in the past. However, it continues to evolve in response to changes in our society. For example, it explores our understanding of science as well as our application of that knowledge through technology. Current steampunk writers, artists, and enthusiasts generally agree that the seeds of the movement come from the works of Victorian-era writers such as Jules Verne, Mary Shelley, and H. G. Wells, perhaps the originators of science fiction. These writers explored what their world would be like if certain as-yet-to-be-invented technologies existed. The actual phrase "steampunk" wasn't used until the 1980s, when writers began to rediscover what might be called "Victorian fantasy." Whether it is Jules Verne or my current favorite steampunk author, Gail Carriger, these authors explore alternative histories or worlds that "might have been." While these stories traditionally have been set in Victorian London, that is changing as authors explore other settings, such as Cherie Priest's *Boneshaker*, which is set in 1880s Seattle.

Much more can, and has, been said about steampunk. If the look appeals to you, I encourage you to explore it further. Behind the great props and costumes and devices lies a whole world of interesting "what ifs." Grab your brass goggles and your best corset or top hat, and join in the adventure.

MORE THAN A NOVELTY DECK?

While many of us are attracted to steampunk because of the aesthetic, is there more to this deck than tarot dressed up in extremely awesome clothing? Can a "steampunk" tarot be more than a novelty deck? I think so.

Steampunk, and any genre or subculture, reflects our current struggles and concerns as a culture. The genre of steampunk itself also shares some fundamental characteristics with tarot. In tarot, many of the cards explore the relationship between opposing energies and the desirability of balancing opposites within ourselves. Some cards even hint at serious issues that occur when our lives are not in balance. This search for balance is part of the spiritual quest that the cards reveal. As you study the images and their correspondences, you'll also be taking a spiritual journey. What is really amazing about tarot is that it does not tout one path. The tarot is not a book. It is not read in a linear fashion. Instead, the cards are shuffled and laid out in a seemingly random order; this is how it can show personal journeys and truths. Because we are all on our own trip in this life—we share some common touchstones and experiences, but no two lives are identical. Just as tarot explores contrary energies, so does steampunk, combining as it does reality and fantasy, magic and machine, facts and imagination.

While the spiritual aspect is an important element of tarot, the most common use of the cards is to read one's fortune. In most readings we intend to examine the past, consider the present, and speculate about the future. That sounds almost like a definition for steampunk, which is set in the past and yet explores different possible futures for the world. More precisely, it experiments with how history would have played out if a few things had been different. This is very similar to the best tarot readings. In the same way, in the sacred environment of a reading, we can imagine what would happen *if...* Doing this helps us see the relationship between causes and effects and helps us to make better decisions about our lives.

Tarot, in general, is well known for helping people see their situation more clearly. One of the most interesting characteristics of this deck in particular, which Aly and I discovered as we worked with various compositions, is the importance of perspective. Steampunk, as a subgenre of science fiction and, more and more, of fantasy, is flavored with an epic sense of drama. We wanted the images to express this energy. Whenever a composition felt too static, we changed the perspective; almost always that brought about the desired effect. This tactic fits nicely with the purpose of tarot: by examining any situation in our lives through the cards, we gain a new point of view. When we see things in a different way, solutions that eluded us before are suddenly clear. For those of you familiar with the traditional Rider-Waite-Smith images, you will see many similarities (they are all intentional) in these cards. You will, we hope, also see those old, beloved scenes with new eyes. May the fresh view facilitate increased understanding and brilliant epiphanies.

We can see old things from new vantage points. We can also look at deeper social truths through the lens of popular culture. It is interesting to watch how different genres rise in popularity, from witches and wizards to vampires to goggled and corseted preternaturals. Historians are trained to track such things and to speculate about the connection between popular culture and what is going on in the world. Although it has been a number of years since I put my master's degree in British history to formal use, I cannot help but notice things. Looked at through the lens of world events, the rise in steampunk's popularity now makes sense. There is a strong focus on technology being not only epic but also part of people's everyday and personal lives. Steampunk fashion incorporates technology. Today, we are constantly connected not merely with computers but smartphones and iPods and the like. And have you noticed how our fashion has adapted to meet our technological needs? Gloves are designed to facilitate texting. Purses and bags as well as coats and jackets have pockets sized to hold our mobile devices.

As fashion adapts to new needs, we explore psychological, social, and other needs through our storytelling. In literature, movies, and TV shows, we (as a culture) explore things that need exploring (such as our relationship with technology, how we negotiate a changing social landscape, feelings of isolation and loneliness in a world where our lives are lived in public, etc.). In tarot, we also explore things that need exploring...what is going on in our lives, what will happen if we do _____ [insert action], how should we respond to _____ [insert situation or feeling]. Humans have always told stories, whether they are about grand events (such as the creation of the world) or small situations (such as how we got stuck in traffic today). Steampunk gives us a unique world in which to set our current stories. Tarot helps us tell the stories of our lives. Through both, we gain understanding, comfort, and advice.

As a genre, steampunk is evolving to keep pace with our interests and concerns. In its earliest forms, it was more strictly a combination of history and science fiction. Now, at least in my opinion, the very best steampunk literature includes the mysterious and magical as well. Since the late seventeenth century, the so-called Age of Reason, Western civilization has shaped its ideas of progress and enlightenment by the guidelines of modern science. Interestingly, the Victorians exhibited a strong attraction to spiritualism, occultism, and the supernatural. Communing with the dead through séances, for example, or the rise of secret societies such as the Order of the Golden Dawn and the Fellowship of the Rosy Cross are a few ways that Victorians sought to explore worlds outside the strictly prescribed reality of "reason." In fact, the Victorian era is responsible for two of the tarot decks that have had the greatest influence on modern tarot: the Rider-Waite Tarot and the Thoth Tarot. In our own age, more and more thinkers, and even scientists, realize that the schema as set forth by the Age of Reason is not the only viable map of reality. The unquantifiable, the immeasurable—at least by our current means—affects our reality in ways that we do not understand. Accepting this unsettling realization by bringing it into our steampunk world makes this fascinating subgenre an even more apropos lab.

It does make sense that the steampunk world resonates with so many of us as a way to explore our changing society and our individual responses to those changes. And it makes sense to me to create a tarot deck that does not merely wear steampunk attire but also connects with and expresses itself through steampunk themes. Throughout the images in this deck, you will see humans and machines, nature and devices, science and alchemy, light and dark, despair and kindness, loss and grace, pain and healing. When considering these opposing energies, experiences, and ideals, look at the space where they meet. There you will see their commonality, which can teach you as much as studying their differences will. Each card is a portal to infinite wisdom. This book can only give you the keys to open the doors. It is up to you to walk through and explore.

A MAP OF YOUR JOURNEY

Everyone who explores tarot finds their own way, eventually developing their own personal relationship with the cards and having their own experiences. However, because the world of tarot is vast—limitless, really—it is helpful to have a map of the terrain. This guide will give you a big-picture view of tarot and the possibilities therein. First, you will learn the necessary basics of tarot in general, such as: What exactly is a tarot deck? Where do the meanings come from? What, precisely, is a tarot reading? How do I learn to read the cards myself? This chapter will answer all those questions and provide activities and practices so that you can become comfortable with the cards and continually improve your understanding and skills.

After a firm foundation is established, the next three chapters will explore the cards one by one. For each card, there will be a black-and-white image of the card being discussed. A short sentence, known in the gaming world as "flavor text," is also included. As a former gamer, I could not resist having a more or less valid excuse to include this little nugget of fun. Flavor text is a line that is included on gaming cards or in rule books that doesn't really have any bearing on actual play but instead adds "flavor," or characterization, to the experience. While traditional flavor text does not usually include anything of importance, I crafted my flavor text to tie in with the card's meaning.

After the flavor text is the core meaning. Most of the core meanings are taken from my book *Tarot for Beginners*. As you will see, the cards have many meanings. However, I believe that they also have a core meaning, from which all meanings come. If the longer meanings feel overwhelming, work with the images themselves and the core meanings until you gain confidence. Then you can gradually increase your tarot card meaning vocabulary.

Following the core meaning, you will find a further exploration of the card. These explorations are just that, meanderings and wanderings inspired by the card, the art, tarot symbolism, or historical tidbits that all enhance the meaning and understanding of the card. One characteristic that you may have noticed about steampunk is that it is quite eclectic. Whereas subcultures such as the Society for Creative Anachronism focus on historical accuracy, steampunk is more like a fertile playground where almost all your favorite interests can come together in ways that somehow make sense. In this section of the card essays, I let myself enjoy that same freedom. To maintain some sense of consistency, each exploration ends with a paragraph to help you weave the card interpretation into your readings.

On some of the card pages you will notice a section called reading tips. These little treasures are sprinkled throughout the text; not all the cards have them. They are helpful hints to help enhance your readings, expand your understanding, see relationships between the cards, or provide more traditional "fortunetelling" meanings for the cards.

Once you have explored and played with the cards, it's time to deal them out and read your fate! A collection of spreads will help you read for nearly any type of question. If you like spreads, are fascinated with creating systems, or like instilling order on chaos, you might want to explore spreads further. If so, my book *Tarot Spreads: Tips and Techniques to Empower Your Readings* might be of interest. It explains the fundamentals of spread design, provides over seventy unique spreads, and teaches you how to create your own spreads.

After that, you will be ready to explore the vast and fascinating world of the cards. Is your bustle in good order or monocle in place? Your snuffbox handy? Parasol at the ready? Let's jump in this zeppelin and see where it takes us!

THE DECK

Fantastic devices and precisely crafted engines feature prominently in steampunk worlds. These creations are not merely examples of visual beauty and technological impressiveness. They perform some useful function and are thereby classified as practical. The tarot is like one of these marvels, for it is not only a visual delight but also a very finely crafted tool. Tools are used to aid in accomplishing tasks. We'll explore some of tarot's uses later in this chapter, but here we'll examine some of its extraordinary design features and their functions.

Your tarot deck is comprised of seventy-eight cards. The deck can be divided into sub-decks. This makes learning the cards easier, because each sub-deck contains cards that have common characteristics. Grouping things always helps make them easier to understand—similar to, for example, asking if an unknown item is an animal, vegetable, or mineral, or identifying something's genus and species.

The first division of the deck is between the Major Arcana and Minor Arcana. Arcana is a lovely old word for "secrets." One part of the deck, then, reveals the big, or major, secrets, while the other part holds the small, or minor, secrets. Both of these sub-decks have their own unique qualities and play different roles in the deck as a whole and in readings.

There are twenty-two cards in the Major Arcana. They are numbered from 0 to 21 and have names like the Fool, the Chariot, Temperance, and the Moon. The images on these cards often date back to tarot's beginnings in the fifteenth century, although some have changed through the centuries. As the "major" cards in the deck, they represent significant influences in our lives. These are the milestones and life lessons of the human experience. When interpreted, they often carry with them deeply spiritual messages. Because they are such powerful forces in a reading, it is often said that they represent events and developments over which we have little control. They are like weather fronts that we cannot alter but can prepare for. They reveal situations such as moving somewhere new, getting married (or divorced), starting a degree program, finding (or losing) faith, or organizing a new business. The Major Arcana is a complete unit and is not further divided.

The fifty-six cards of the Minor Arcana represent the nuts and bolts of everyday life. In these cards we find things like balancing the budget, arguing with coworkers, being recognized for an accomplishment, finding a new romance, starting an exciting project, and even feeling bored. The minor cards are further divided into four groups: wands, cups, swords, and pentacles. These are the four suits of the tarot. Each of the suits is associated with different aspects of our lives. Wands are careers, projects, passions, and, most importantly, our will. Cups illustrate our emotional experiences and relationships. Swords show us our challenges and our ways of thinking. Pentacles represent the physical aspects of life. We'll go into much more depth about the suits as we examine the cards in chapter 3. Each suit has fourteen cards: ace through ten and a page, knight, queen, and king.

The ace through ten cards are sometimes called the numbered cards or the pips, although technically pip cards are not illustrated, as the cards of the Steampunk Tarot are. Instead, traditional pip cards are adorned with suit designators, like the ones in a pack of playing cards. The pages, knights, queens, and kings are called the court cards. These are sometimes subdivided and separated from the numbered cards because they represent not events or situations but people. These cards signify the person asking the question in a reading or other people involved or affecting the question. In this book we'll look at all the court cards together, as they are easier to classify when examined as a group.

The tarot deck is indeed a finely crafted tool, with cards designated to signify all aspects of the human experience, from the beginning of life to the end (and, some would say, beyond), from the highest spiritual aspirations to the most mundane necessities, from one's self to family and friends and anyone affecting one's life. There are cards devoted to our intellect, our will, our feelings, and our bodies. The cards all have meanings—indeed, often many layers of meanings. The elements of the cards, such as the names, numbers, and suits, are also designed to help make reading them easier, which we shall soon see.

As far as we know, tarot cards were originally created in the fifteenth century and used to play a trick-taking game (like bridge). Tarot history is actually more complicated than this sentence indicates. Tarot evolved from other types of decks from other parts of the world. They did not simply appear fully formed and out of the context of playing-card history. If you are interested in the history of tarot, read Robert Place's *The Tarot: History, Symbolism, and Divination*. Given tarot's amazingly useful and versatile structure, one would be tempted to think that perhaps this thing we call tarot was not simply a popular card game turned spiritual tool but something more, guided by the hand of some wise and beneficent force.

USES

Alton Brown (of the cooking show *Good Eats*) always eschews kitchen tools that he calls "one-trick ponies." He simply does not have room in his kitchen or his life for something so specialized that it can only be used for one task. Instead, he looks for clever, well-built tools that can be put to multiple uses. While I'm not sure Mr. Brown is into metaphysics, if he were, I'm sure he'd approve of tarot, for it is certainly no one-trick pony.

As mentioned earlier, the original use of tarot was entertainment. The cards were used to play a game, and in many parts of the world, particularly Europe, the game is still played. In Italy it is so common that the cards are sold in tobacco shops and newsstands. On any corner, you can pick up a deck of tarot cards, go to the closest sidewalk café, and play a hand or two with a friend.

In the United States (and probably Canada, Britain, and Australia), the most common use of the cards is for doing a reading, and in a few paragraphs we'll spend a significant amount of time talking about how to do readings. In fact, you probably picked up this kit because you are interested in learning to "read the cards," meaning that you want to use the cards to peek at the foreseeable future. There are other things we can do within the context of a reading besides glimpsing our fortune. These "other things" make doing readings even more useful and far more interesting.

These days tarotists, also known as tarot readers or tarot enthusiasts, use the cards in many ways. The images are great for brainstorming. Any one card can be used as a journaling prompt. Magical folk use the cards in spells and in magic of all sorts. Pagans and other spiritually inclined people incorporate the cards in rituals. Writers use the cards to create plots, develop characters, and overcome writer's block. Artists use the structure of the deck as a foundation for creative expression. Psychologists weave the symbols and archetypes of the cards into their sessions. The cards can be used as a focal point for meditation. Bringing tarot full circle, tarot is even used in modern role-playing games. *Brass and Steel* (www.pameangames.com) incorporates tarot as part of the rules governing play.

If you are the creative, adventurous type (and really, aren't all steampunkers adventurous?), you can easily imagine ways to use the cards in any or all of these ways. But there is nothing wrong, even for adventurers, with learning from those who have gone before. There is not room in this humble work to cover all these uses. However, one of my earlier books, *What Tarot Can Do for You*, provides guidance for alternative uses. Using that wonderful device called Google will point you in the direction of many excellent tarot blogs where the authors generously share their ideas and techniques. For now, though, we'll focus here on readings.

ANATOMY OF A READING

Ask three readers to describe what happens during a reading and you'll get three different answers. Actual readings depend quite heavily on the beliefs of the reader and are also influenced by the querent (the person asking the question and getting the reading), the question asked, the spread selected, and the deck used. At its most basic level, a reading is when someone consults the cards for guidance. Beyond that, there is plenty of room to personalize your readings by incorporating your beliefs and your reading style. You already know what you believe about the nature of the universe, the future, and free will. If not, check out the questions below and see if they help you clarify your thinking. As for your reading style, that will develop over time. Some of the activities at the end of this chapter will encourage you to play with cards and thereby uncover the approaches that resonate with you.

The nature of a tarot reading is very dependent on what you, as the tarot reader, think about the way the world works. There are questions that cannot be answered with complete and utter certainty; they are matters of belief and faith. But they are important questions, such as:

1. Can the future be told, and if so, to what extent?

2. Where does the information gleaned in a tarot reading come from—the reader's mind? The querent's subconscious? The hand of the Divine?

3. What is the role of the tarot reader—a guide for the querent? A voice for the gods? An interpreter of symbols? A teller of stories? A creator of the future?

4. Is a reader obliged to tell the querent everything he or she sees in the reading, or should the reader keep some things back? How does the reader determine what to share or what to withhold?

5. Are any types of questions or subjects off-limits?

Those are just a few of the heady questions that tarot dredges up! And they spawn more questions. While considering all the possible answers and ramifications would be quite a bit of fun, we do have some space limitations here. Instead, I will detail how I do readings and include my reasoning, when appropriate, as well as point out possible different options or opinions. You can measure my practices and supporting logic against yours, and simply modify them to suit your tastes.

As for me, I think predicting the future is very much like predicting the weather. When we consult a weather report, the forecast for the next day is likely pretty reliable, but the seven-day forecast is more apt to change. Weather forecasts are based on complicated equations with many variables. The further out you look, the greater the chance that one of those variables will vary, thereby causing a change in the outcome. And so it is with our future—and our tarot readings.

There are trends and fronts and forces that shape the direction of events in a person's life. A tarot reading gives a clear picture of what the future looks like based on the moment that the reading is done. However, because people have free will, actions can be taken to shift energies and change, to some extent and in some cases, the future. Things do change and small actions can create significantly different futures. Certain aspects of the future are more difficult to change. Again, this is not only because you have free will, but other people have free will also. They may make decisions or take actions that are contrary to what you desire. Also, I believe there are things that the Divine allows to happen for your benefit and for the greatest good of all. These experiences set in motion by the Divine are not arbitrary. They are designed in conjunction with your soul before your incarnation in this life. Sometimes we cannot see how something is for our benefit until years later. A skilled reader can tell the story of the upcoming trends as well as advise the querent about energy flows that can or cannot be changed, and explore options to achieve desired goals within the existing situation. This, in a nutshell, is my philosophy of tarot reading. Yours may very well be different.

The information gained in a reading is a creation by the querent, the Divine, and me. We all bring our knowledge and sensibilities to the table. As a reader, I offer not only my symbol-interpreting skills but also my psychic connection with the Divine, which I try to keep open and clear through meditation, self-reflection, and humility. This is clearly my personal approach and certainly not necessary for doing an effective reading and definitely not practiced by all readers. In my readings the querent, the Divine, and I work together to both foretell and create the future. It's really very exciting, empowering, and awesome.

In addition to blending in your own beliefs, your readings will evolve to reflect your personal style. Readings can be as simple or as complex as you like...a casual glance at the cards or a full-scale event! At its most basic, a reading requires a deck of tarot cards, a question, and someone to interpret the cards. You have your deck of cards and you will interpret them. But what about the question? The question needn't be a fully formed, ultraprecise sentence, unless you want it to be. Here are some examples of different types of questions, all of which would be considered a valid question for a reading by some readers.

1. Will I get a boyfriend soon?

2. Is my husband cheating on me?

3. How can I find the right job for me at this time?

4. What do I need to know about my relationship?

5. Do I have cancer? Will the test come back positive?

6. When will I get married?

7. Will I ever have a baby?

8. Should I marry Susan?

9. Why isn't Mark returning my calls?

10. What does the universe want me to know right now?

11. Is the spirit communicating with me through my dreams benevolent or evil?

Some of these questions are simply seeking information. Some are designed to provide advice. My favorite readings are ones that do both: get a clear idea of what is happening as well as what is likely to happen, and then create an action plan. Think about what you would most like to ask the cards. Experiment with different types of questions. One last piece of advice: don't ask if you don't really want to know the answer, whatever that answer is. Before doing a reading, imagine a wide range of possible answers. What would your response be to any one of them? How would that answer affect your life or shape your decisions?

While you are pondering the ramifications of your questions, let's consider additional possible reading practices. We'll look at an outline for a full-blown reading, an event that may be more like a ritual than most people's definition of a reading. Think of it as a reading buffet. You can take a little of everything, or none of something, or even seconds of something else. It's your plate. You can fill it however you like.

Space

It used to be that in order to read the cards, you needed at least a flat surface on which to lay the cards. To use this deck, that is still true. However, with more and more apps available, you can read anytime and anywhere with a virtual deck. That can be a convenient option, but most readers I know love the tactile experience of shuffling and handling the cards. For those of us who prefer paper to bytes, we still need a space. Minimally, that means enough room to lay out the cards needed for the reading and, one hopes, a clean enough area so that the cards do not get sticky, warped, or stained.

Some people want more than that. They think of a reading as a communication with the Divine, a sacred act. In reaching out to the Divine, they wish to create a liminal space, a time out of time, a place out of place, a world between worlds. This can be helpful in many ways, both magical and mundane. If you are a magical practitioner, then you know that creating a sacred space or casting a circle does benefit any magic or sacred work. Even if you are a muggle, you might wish to harness the psychological benefit of creating a special reading space. By making an area feel out of the ordinary, it lets the mind know you are entering a place where something special and unexpected can happen. It helps you (and your querent, if you are reading for someone else) be more open to insights, which is the reason you are conducting the reading.

Because I think of a reading as an act of observing as well as creating the future, I consider a reading to be a magical act. Most tarot readers and magical folk know the saying "as above, so below." This is a Hermetic principle that means whatever happens in spirit happens in the world, and vice versa. It is often seen as a magical or spiritual version of microcosm and macrocosm—that is, you and the universe, respectively. It is one of the ways that magic works. You make a change within yourself and change the world. Or you do a spell using items that represent realities in the world and spiritual plane and thereby create change. At a Pagan conference in the summer of 2011, John Michael Greer spoke of sacred spaces as being mesocosms. A mesocosm is something that is used primarily to study aquatic ecosystems. It is a small environment created to mimic a larger environment. In it, experiments can be conducted safely, without ramifications in the "real" world. Greer posited that sacred spaces can be thought of as mesocosms, places to experiment with possible actions and see possible responses. I think of a tarot reading as a mesocosm. A reading is a place to experiment with reality—testing out actions, decisions, and approaches—and to examine and assess results and possible futures. Considering that this is done while accessing the guidance and requesting the wisdom of the Divine, creating a bit of sacred space would certainly be appropriate.

How one creates sacred space is highly personal. Again, magic folks may opt to cast a full circle. Other ways to create instant special space include laying out a nice cloth (plain works better than patterned because patterns compete visually with the card images), lighting a candle or incense, or setting out a few favorite crystals or sacred items. Any magic user will tell you that intent is the most important aspect of any magic, so remember that nothing is precisely necessary. Sacred space can exist and be entered at any time if that is what you intend to do.

Ritual

Related to sacred space is the idea of ritual. Like sacred space, ritual can be used for magical purposes or for psychological reasons. As magical practitioners can attest, ritual acts and words acquire power and energy over time. Every time you perform a ritual act, you tap into the energy generated by every past performance of that ritual. Depending on the purpose of the ritual, that energy can be used, for example, to enhance divinatory clarity or create change in your life. However, there are other, more mundane benefits to incorporating ritual into your reading practice. By "ritual" I mean any act that is done regularly, generally at the same point within a reading, and in the same way. With this very loose definition, we can fit many different actions into this classification. Very simple rituals include starting every reading with the same phrase, such as words of welcome to the querent or words of gratitude to the Divine, or simply using the same process to shuffle and cut the cards before a reading. A simple "ground and center" practice or three slow, deep breaths are simple ways to signal the start of a reading and also quiet your energy so you can focus more easily. Readers sometimes use longer or more elaborate rituals, such as laying out tokens of each of the four suits in tarot or doing a specific meditation. I know one reader who simply taps her tarot deck three times with one finger before each reading. Any act can become a ritual.

Whatever type of ritual you prefer, one benefit is that ritual trains your mind to know that something specific is about to happen—in this case, a reading. Every time you complete the ritual, you psychologically prepare to enter a state suitable for interpreting the cards. That state will vary from person to person, depending on your beliefs and approach to reading. Another benefit may or may not be true, but it feels true to me; you can decide for yourself. It is an idea based on recent research about the idea of self-depleting control. Current studies show that a person has a finite amount of will or energy for self-control and that this energy is directly related to making good or healthy choices. With each decision made, the individual's store is depleted, leading to less and less wise choices. My reasoning is that the more actions within a reading that are done by rote (thereby eliminating the need to make decisions), the more energy and focus the reader can bring to the actual interpretation of the cards. Finally, any act of ritual works with the idea of creating sacred space, or sacred time, and enhances the reading experience.

Practical Concerns

Some reading preferences are more practical than the ideas of sacred space and ritual. For example, how should one shuffle the cards? You should shuffle your cards however you like, in whatever way feels comfortable for you. Truly, there are no right and wrong ways to shuffle a tarot deck. Pick up your cards and try riffling them. Then try the overhand method. If you are so inclined, do a quick mud pie—put the deck face-down on the table and just smear the cards all over, swirling and mixing them like mud or finger paint. Gather them up and manipulate them back together in a neat pack. What felt right? What was the most fun?

Will you let someone else shuffle or otherwise handle your cards? Some readers have the querent shuffle the cards, because for them it is how the querent's energy enters the reading. Other readers do not want anyone else to touch their cards, either because they do not want other energy mixed in or because querents tend to get anxious when asked to shuffle, worried about "doing it wrong." An anxious querent, they say, is harder to read for, so instead they shuffle the cards while engaging the querent in conversation about the reading.

After the cards are shuffled, some readers cut the cards. I was taught to cut the deck into three piles using my non-dominant hand. While I do not think it is the "right" or only way to prepare the cards for a reading, I like to shuffle the cards myself and then ask the querent to cut the cards in this way, mostly to let them be involved in the preparation without making them anxious or uncomfortable. Some readers cut the cards in two piles—or five piles—or not at all. It is all part of the ritual of preparing for a reading. My advice, as always, is to do what feels right to you. But beyond simply what feels right, remember that tarot is very symbolic, so let whatever you do within the context of your reading have meaning. It adds depth to your reading practice.

The cards are finally prepared, shuffled, and cut in accordance to your preferences. Now it is time to lay them out on the table. The manner in which you lay them out is called a spread. We will talk more about spreads in chapter 5. Spreads are diagrams that show you where to place the cards and what the card in any particular position means. For example, a simple spread is this popular Past-Present-Future Spread.

1 2 3

1. This card indicates what happened in the past that is influencing the current situation.

2. This card represents the present energies at play in the situation.

3. This card shows the probable outcome if everything stays as it is now.

A spread is usually selected before the cards are shuffled. Some readers use the same spread for every reading, such as the Celtic Cross or some variation of the Horseshoe Spread. Others use different spreads depending on the question asked. Still others invent their own spreads on the spot for every reading.

Whatever spread you decide to use, you need to lay the cards down. It is a very simple act, but it still involves a decision. Do you lay the cards face-up or face-down? People who lay them face-down do so for the following reasons: turning the cards face-up one at a time creates a sense of drama and tension. Also, looking at the cards one at a time allows the reader and the querent to focus on that card and not be distracted by, say, the Tower or the Two of Cups in the future position.

While I understand that reasoning, I prefer to lay the cards face-up. As you will see in the next section, looking at all the cards at once, face-up, before interpreting individual cards plays an important role in the reading. Note your immediate, gut-feeling preference, but withhold final judgment until you have finished reading this chapter and have tried both ways for yourself.

Related to the idea of laying cards face-up or face-down is the concept of reversed cards. In traditional fortunetelling books, meanings were always given for reversed cards, and readers were encouraged to make sure they shuffled in such a way as to create reversed cards in their decks. Reversed cards are ones that show up in your reading upside down. While reversals are definitely part of the tarot-reading tradition, today just as many readers use them as don't. I myself have had a long history with reversals. I had to devise a system and use it when I went through my certification fifteen years ago. I never liked using them, but I force myself to try reading reversals every year or so just to make sure I still don't like them. Except for a brief fling with them a few years ago, I do not read reversals. Reading the cards is, to me, a very visual experience. The images are created to be read upright. Instead of reversals, I rely on other cards in the spread, other techniques (which we will cover in the next section), and my intuition to narrow down the meaning of the card for a particular reading.

Reversals never clicked with me because the traditional reversed meanings never seemed to make sense in terms of either the upright meaning or the image. They were just so arbitrary. One reason I love tarot is that it is a complete and logical system. This structure creates a trustworthy and effective foundation that lets my left brain relax so my right brain can connect with the images more easily. Throwing in a "system" that makes no rational sense didn't add to my ability to read the cards; in fact, it detracted from it. Because I do not use them, I do not have the experience to draw on to create reversed meanings to share with you. Consequently, this book does not provide reversed meanings. If you already read reversed cards, then simply apply your own philosophy or interpretations. If you are interested in reversals, I encourage you to explore them in other books or online. Consider what they mean theoretically and apply that to the cards rather than memorizing arbitrary definitions. In particular, I recommend Mary K. Greer's *Complete Book of Tarot Reversals*.

Working with the tarot really is such a rich experience, just as exploring or working within the steampunk genre is layered and textured, creating plenty of opportunity for inventiveness. Steampunkers revel in a hands-on approach to discovery. They see possibilities and express their creativity through exploring and adapting anything and everything to suit their needs. Like the finely crafted devices of the Victorian era, tarot cards are beautiful treasures that fit in the palm of your hand and play the practical role of containing layers of meaning and wisdom. Your readings will showcase your spiritual and psychological beliefs and reflect your personal style as you try out ideas for creating just the right space, incorporating rituals, finding your favorite shuffling method, and experimenting with reversals. In the next section, I'll share some techniques that have helped with my study of the cards and improved my reading practice.

D.I.Y. TECHNIQUES

Thinking about important spiritual, psychological, and symbolic issues is a crucial part of tarot reading. But let's face it: there are many other ways to reflect on these issues and many other forms of divination. Most of us who love tarot also love the feel of the cards in our hands. Shuffling. Laying them out. Flipping them over. Moving them around. Diving into the stories they reveal. In this section we will talk about actually using the cards, including my favorite reading techniques and ways to perfect your style.

If you are a steampunker, you already know that the DIY ethic is a strong part of the genre. Punkers are not ones to take ready-made anything as the final word. They cut and stitch and weld and embellish until they've made it thoroughly and completely their own. The same is true for tarot in general, because if something doesn't resonate with you, it's just not right. Use that same principle, the one that says "make it your own," here. You can approach this section in any number of ways. You can try these exercises as you read them, without referencing the card meanings given in the next chapter. This is a great way to immediately connect with the images intuitively. You can read through all of the card meanings and then come back to the activities. You can do the activities and consult the card meanings simultaneously. Personally, I am a "read the interpretations first" type of girl by nature, so I fully understand that desire. However, it is fun (and enlightening!) to shake things up a bit and just dive in.

Telling Stories

The first step in learning to read the cards is cultivating your inner story teller. The meanings of the cards are just one part of tarot, which we will cover in the next chapter.

In some ways, it seems like it is the easier part. Putting the meanings together in a way that makes sense is sometimes more challenging. Having a profound understanding of the cards does not necessarily mean one knows how to weave them together to create a rich, meaningful tapestry.

One of the challenges is that we forget how to tell stories based on pictures. As children, this is no problem. But when I lay three cards in front of an adult and say, "Just tell me what you see; what is the story?" she freezes and seems to be afraid she'll get it wrong or make some embarrassing mistake. There is nothing to worry about. There is no way you can get this part wrong. Pick up your cards. Shuffle them. Lay out three cards in a horizontal row. The first card is the beginning of the story. The second is the middle. The third is the ending. Now, tell yourself the story that you see. If you feel stuck or frozen, start by simply describing what you see in excruciating detail. Then guess at how that scene came to be and imagine what might happen next.

Another way to practice seeing stories in the cards is a technique that I learned in the early 1990s from tarot author Sasha Fenton. In her book *Super Tarot* she explains her technique, which is "to work in a completely back-to-front manner by choosing the cards which will illustrate a particular story. The point of this approach is to encourage you to think about the cards in logical groups" to describe the story that you want told.

Right now, think of what happened to you yesterday and go through your cards. Select one or two or even three that illustrate the situation you have in mind. If your life doesn't inspire you, pick a movie you just saw or a book you recently read and select cards that tell that story.

One Card, Many Meanings

Many tarot enthusiasts begin by studying the cards, reading all they can about them. Learning about all the fascinating nuances and correspondences creates a firm foundation for understanding the cards. However, once in the midst of an actual reading, you realize that all that theory is only the beginning. After learning about the core identity of the card, you then have to learn how to interpret it in the context of the reading. Below are some techniques that you can do before reading the card meanings or after, whichever is most comfortable for you. If you try this without reading the interpretations, I bet you will be surprised to see how well you do just by looking at the images.

A card's core meaning explains the essence of the card. However, simply quoting the meaning to any and all questions will not make for a very coherent reading. All cards do have a base meaning, but the cards also have many facets. There are many factors that influence what aspect of the card you will draw into your reading. Three of the most common are the position of a card in a spread, the question asked, and the querent. The three activities that follow highlight each of these influences.

Below is a list of questions that could represent the position in a spread. Pick one card and use that same card to answer all of them. You will see how easy it is to find the right facet to apply to any situation and how the position affects the card interpretation.

- What is my greatest strength?

- What is my biggest weakness?

- What is my current challenge?

- What will help me?

- What do I love?

- What do I fear?

- What do I need to release?

- What should I do today?

- What should I buy _____ for their birthday?

- When will I _____ [fill in the blank with something you want to do or accomplish]?

A common use for tarot is to seek advice. In fact, "advice" is a very common position in many spreads. But the type of advice will vary depending on the question asked. To get an idea of how this works, pull a single card from your deck and interpret it as advice for someone asking the following questions:

- Will I get a job soon?

- Will I find love?

- How can I find my highest spiritual path?

- How can I improve my relationship with my boss?

- What can I do about my marriage? Something seems off.

The person getting a reading also affects the card interpretation. Select a card. Read it as advice in a reading about how to find love or romance. Imagine you are reading for the following people and see how you might interpret the card differently for each of them:

- Yourself

- Your best friend

- Your sibling

- Someone you dislike

- A 23-year-old woman just starting a challenging but promising new career

- A 48-year-old man, recently divorced, with three children in shared custody; things are not smooth between him and his ex

- A 68-year-old woman, widowed three years after a twenty-five-year happy marriage

- A 25-year-old woman, widowed less than one year after marrying

- A 32-year-old man who just lost his job and hasn't been in a relationship in five years

These techniques will help you quickly become comfortable interpreting any card in any situation. Here is a little warning for you: some books may advocate the use of "clarifier" cards. These are extra cards drawn when a reader cannot figure out how to interpret the card that turned up in the actual reading. I encourage you to shun that practice. It will, in my opinion, make you a lazy reader and create a muddled reading. If a card comes up and you do not understand right away what it means, remember: it showed up for a reason. Sit with it until you understand. Take the card through these exercises: what does it mean in the position, in relation to the question, and in relation to the querent?

PRACTICE MAKES PERFECT

When you get ready to do full readings, you'll want plenty of practice. After all, practice does make perfect. With each reading you do, your confidence will grow. Try these ideas for getting in as much experience as possible.

1: Read for Yourself

This has limitations, of course. Reading for yourself can be challenging simply because it is harder to be objective. Another hazard of reading for yourself is that you will read in a haphazard manner, not putting as much effort into it as if you were reading for someone else. An excellent way to avoid that pitfall is to make an audio recording of your reading and then listen to it right away. Also, recording and reviewing your readings helps you see your strengths and identify any areas that need work. In the end, it will help you be a better reader.

2: Read for Friends and Family

Usually once they know you're offering free readings, you'll have plenty of volunteers. Again, this can be tricky since you have to read what the cards say, not what *you* want to say!

3: Read for Imaginary Querents

Invent a person with a short bio and create a question or read for a fictional character. This option is problematic for some people. They say that a reading is a sacred connection with the Divine and to read in this way is disrespectful. As for me, I also believe that it is a sacred act. However, my concept of the Divine is quite benevolent (think Ganesha), and it wants me to be as skilled as possible, so I believe it does not begrudge me a little practice time.

4: Pretend a Celebrity Has Asked for a Reading and Practice on Them

This is a great option because you can do your reading and then watch the tabloids to see how the situation unfolds, allowing you to gauge the accuracy of your readings. However, it may cross ethical boundaries for some people. One of the ethical decisions you must make is whether or not you will read about people without their permission. Even readers who take that stance tend to lighten up a bit on the celebrity issue, especially when the readings are for your eyes only. Likewise, you can read for any current event.

5: Take a Hint from the Telling Stories Technique

Before going to a movie or before watching the next episode of your favorite weekly show, do a reading to see what will happen.

6: Read for the Cards

This technique riffs off suggestion number 3 and actually packs a double punch in terms of learning the cards. Select one of the court cards to represent an imaginary querent. Pull another card to represent the situation or question. If desired, pull another court card to represent another person involved in the situation. This is particularly useful in practicing relationship readings.

MY NOT-SO-SECRET
READING TECHNIQUE

As I've said, perhaps too many times, you will eventually develop your own style and your own methods of reading the cards. It is good to have a jumping-off point, though, so I'll give a step-by-step account of how I do a reading. We'll assume the space has been cleared and blessed, I'm grounded, the question and spread have been selected, and the cards are shuffled and laid out.

Before digging into the details of a reading, I like to get an overview. Looking at the big picture helps me relate the details in the cards to a larger framework, creating a more coherent message. I think of it as an artist first sketching out a composition and then filling in the details. The sketch helps keep everything in perspective and in proper relation. The details give the image nuance and bring it to life.

1: Look for Major Arcana Cards

The majors make up fewer than one-third of the deck. If more than 30 percent of the cards in a reading are majors, this tells me that there are larger forces at work in this situation than usual. Likely the question hits on something bigger than the querent realizes. Major Arcana cards indicate life lessons and longer time frames, issues that you can blend into your overall interpretation. Also, there are probably more forces or energies or events happening that are beyond the querent's control.

2: Look for the Court Cards

Less than one-quarter of the cards are court cards. If more than 25 percent show up in a reading, keep in mind that there may be many other people involved or influencing the situation. Another possibility is that the querent is feeling torn about how to behave or is having identity issues.

3: Analyze the Suits Present

Are all four suits equally represented? If not, what is predominant and how might that influence the energy of the situation? What is missing? Is that suit one that should be brought into the situation by the querent? You can find out more about the suits' energy and characteristics at the beginning of each suit's section in chapter 3: page 115 for wands, page 145 for cups, page 175 for swords, and page 203 for pentacles.

I don't always expect the suits to be equally represented. For example, I would expect more cups in a reading about relationships than in one about a job hunt. What is striking to me is when there are no cups present in, say, a romance reading. When a reading is about a job or career, it is interesting to determine the querent's priorities by the suits present. Pentacles is financial, of course. Wands shows that ambition and excitement are valued. Swords indicates a love of problem-solving and analysis. Cups suggests that emotional fulfillment and good relations with coworkers and clients matter a lot to this querent.

4: Check the Numbers

When beginning a study of tarot, one of the first things students learn about is correspondences. For some reason, tarotists love (and the cards lend themselves to) correspondences. Correspondences are other systems or symbols that, well, correspond to tarot cards. Common pairings include astrology and tarot as well as Kabbalah and tarot. As for me, I don't use those very often. However, I do tend to use some numerological correspondences, particularly with the numbered cards of the Minor Arcana, to add to the reading's overall theme and to ascertain where in process a situation is.

These are general meanings that, over time, I've come to associate with the numbers.

Aces: new beginnings

Twos: duality, balance, relationship, choices

Threes: creativity, nurturing

Fours: stability, structure, organization, stagnation

Fives: conflict, loss, chaos, opportunity

Sixes: communication, problem-solving

Sevens: reflection, assessment

Eights: movement, speed, power

Nines: compromises, possible stagnation, satiation

Tens: completion, ending a cycle

If there are more than one of any particular number, I consider that number as influencing the theme of the reading. For example, if there are more two or more twos (the Two of Cups and the Two of Swords, for example) present, the issue of choices or decision-making is significant. If two or more eights are present, this tells me that things are moving or developing quickly.

To ascertain where a situation is in development, I scan the numbers in a spread. If there are several:

Aces, twos, and threes: a situation is in the early stages of development

Fours, fives, and sixes: a situation is in the
middle phase

Sevens, eights, and nines: the situation is near
the end

Tens: the situation is all but complete and over

I find this particularly useful. I believe that we have some
control over our lives but not total and complete control. I
also believe that the earlier the stage of development, the
easier it is to change course. So if I am looking at a relationship, where the querent has just begun dating someone, it
is easier for her to affect change in the direction and course
of that relationship. If it is the week before the wedding,
it will be harder for her—for any number of reasons—to
change course.

5: Look at the Visual Pattern Made by the Cards

Tarot is a visual medium. Art and artistic elements matter to most readers. Before looking at the art of each individual card, I look at the cards on the table as if they were
one picture. I look at the colors and shapes. In particular,
I look for a sense of flow. More importantly, I look for the
lack of flow. Most people come for readings because they
have a problem or a challenge. Consequently, the visual lack
of flow often gives a clue about what is causing the block-
age. Then you can look at the surrounding cards for energies that can be used to eliminate the obstruction.

6: Interpret the Cards

After using steps 1 through 5 to create a preliminary sketch, I interpret the individual cards using the given meanings as well as incorporating the techniques from Telling Stories (page 32) and One Card, Many Meanings (page 34).

7: Wrap Up

Most readings reveal so much information that it may be hard to remember it all. Recording your readings, whether in a journal or as an audio file, can be useful. If you are reading for someone else, try to sum up the core of the reading in a sentence or two. I like to give a few action steps whenever appropriate.

Now that you've had a chance to connect with your cards intuitively, let's explore the traditional meanings for the cards and in particular the nuances that steampunkery brings to the images. We'll begin with the Fool, a very apt card, as it represents the beginning of a journey into the unknown. Keep your cards handy, don your goggles, and enjoy the ride. *Allons-y!*

Chapter 2
MAJOR ARCANA

0, THE FOOL

• • • •

**"Up here, everything
looks a little magical."**

Core meaning: The moment
before the first step is taken.

As with all cards marking beginnings and endings in the
tarot, the Fool card is filled with conundrums and contra-
dictions. The sweep, our Fool, is at the beginning, an inno-
cent with no life experience and no wisdom—at least not
the kind of wisdom or experiences this world values. He is
looked down upon, perhaps jeered at. Yet our sweep, and
most Fools in the tarot, is pictured above the world, looking
down on our reality as if from another plane.

The Fool is the soul at the beginning of its journey in this life. More accurately, it is the soul just before stepping into this life, a mere moment before the beginning. Before the Fool jumps down from the heavens into his new life, anything is possible. Once he jumps, the direction is chosen and the adventure begins!

It is said that the soul contains all knowledge, wisdom, and experience that it has gained over various lifetimes and that the soul selects certain lives in order to learn lessons. To achieve its goals, it willfully and voluntarily forgets all, or almost all, that it learned in previous lives. Although it comes into this world ignorant, it does have a destiny. It is seeking something. The soul, which comes to this earth in human form (as a friend of mine says, we are spirit seeking a human experience), contains within it a light that guides its way. We will see this light, symbolized in different ways, throughout the cards; for example, in the Hermit, the Star, Judgement, and the Ten of Wands. This light within guides us so that we stay on the right path, living the life we were meant to live and becoming the people we are meant to become, and leads us, eventually, home.

The light that helps the Fool find his way home exists in the form of a little white dog, a faithful companion who both warns of danger and eagerly leads toward happy adventures.

When the Fool comes to your life in a reading, he lets you know that you are about to embark on a journey that plays an important role in your soul's experience in this world. This card represents decisions that may seem foolish to others and maybe even to you. But you must follow your inner light and listen to your inner little white dog. It will lead you where you need to go and often by a most scenic route. You won't necessarily get a map and itinerary for this journey; you just have to jump in. Get ready and enjoy the ride.

• • • •

Reading tip: The idea of fresh starts and new beginnings in the Fool is emphasized if one or more of the aces or pages are also present. The suits of these cards can give an indication of the pertinent area of life. Coupled with one or more of the knights, the Chariot, the Eight of Cups, or the Six of Swords, travel can be indicated.

I, THE MAGICIAN

• • • •

**"Magic is always there.
Learn to feel it."**

Core meaning: Using knowledge, resources,
and will to create change in the world.

You didn't see all the hours—the long days and nights over many months—that he spent studying the ancient texts, conducting experiments, learning the qualities and characters of the elements, and fine-tuning his techniques. You see the moment it all comes together, when all that work culminates as he feels the energy gather above his head, swirling, intensifying. He and magic are one. He has manifested change in the world according to his will.

The Magician is a master of magic. He has learned to sense the energy of the universe and has become adept at directing it. These skills allow him to accomplish nearly impossible tasks in a way that appears effortless. Don't be fooled, though. He acquired those skills through discipline and practice. The accomplishments are more than the results of mere hard work. They contain an unidentifiable *something*. Think of two piano players. One is technically perfect and sounds quite amazing. The other is also technically perfect and sounds...otherworldly. The second player has tapped into the magical energy of the universe and encourages that energy to swirl in and around and

through everything he does. That energy lifts the work from the merely perfect to the divine.

When you receive the Magician in your reading, it is time to make some magic in your life. Creating magic requires, first and foremost, an understanding of your will. You must know what it is you want to create. Second, you will need to bring your very best skills into play. Third, magic requires connection with the universe and the energies involved. The secret in this card is that you already have all of that: will, skills, and connection. Recognize and use the resources at your disposal. If your faith in yourself is faltering, this card shows up to remind you of how skilled you are and how powerful the universe is. Together—well, together you are magic.

• • • •

Reading tip: Older traditions speak of the negative aspect of the Magician as the con man. If cards such as the Devil, the Five of Swords, the Seven of Swords, or the Moon are present, keep an eye out for trickery or deception.

II, THE HIGH PRIESTESS

• • • •

*"She's completely batty, I tell you.
Didn't say a word that whole time.
Just sat there smiling at me."*

Core meaning: Something that can only
be understood through experience.

Seated before a rich curtain and between curious black and white pillars, she beckons you to her table, smiling mischievously. As you sit, the gears on the pillars quietly begin turning. You are almost hypnotized by the twin infinity symbols formed by the wheels and belts. Before you even ask a question, cards are already face-down on the table. The crystal ball comes to life, mists swirling and lights twinkling within the solid orb, as she runs her gloved hand gently over its surface.

The curtain ripples. The scent of something…pomegranate?…floats on the almost imperceptible breeze. The cards are turned over one by one. Covered with strange images and ancient symbols, they intrigue you. Shapes form within the crystal ball, changing, waxing and waning, conveying truths that resonate in your heart but refuse to be organized into words. You look at her, silently requesting information and clarification. In response, she points at a card, raising an eyebrow, one side of her mouth lifting in a knowing and slightly mocking smile.

People usually come to a tarot reading to have the veil lifted and the truth revealed. The High Priestess symbolizes truth and wisdom and understanding. The maddening thing about her, though, is that she represents the kind of knowing that cannot be told and refuses to be confined to the restrictions of order and language. The logical left brain does not comprehend her intuitive wisdom, nor can it express it. High Priestess truths reside in the heart and soul and can only be learned via direct experience. It is the wisdom gained through an initiatory experience. It cannot be explained or studied. It is simply known.

When the High Priestess beckons you, do not give way to frustration. Curb your left brain that demands understanding, enlightenment, and, above all, answers. She is here to let you know that overt answers are not in your best interest at this time in this situation. You have wisdom to gain and truths to embrace. You will only be able to do so by going through this experience without knowledge of what is to come. Sometimes you have to fly blind. Have faith that the universe has your back. Do your best, and pay attention.

III, THE EMPRESS

· · · ·

"Were you looking for a mother figure?"

Core meaning: Abundance and creation.

Queen Victoria held many titles, including Empress of India. Throughout her reign, her actual role changed. Toward the end, she was almost more of a figurehead than a political leader. She symbolized an era, a way of life, and a tribute to the progress of the human spirit (as it was understood at that time). She was much more than a worldly leader. Likewise, in this card the title, Empress, implies a political role; however, this card's true focus is the laws of the natural world and physical manifestation. In tarot decks, she is often likened to Mother Nature and pictured in an outdoor setting, queen of the flora and fauna.

Here, we scratch a little below the surface of that serene image and access a more primal aspect of the Empress. Instead of the verdant green of nature, we have the rich red of passion, blood, and life. Cycles—of life and death, of creation and destruction, of flower and seed, of the moon and seasons—are intimately connected to the Empress's purview. As indicated by the sign of Venus on the pillow at her side, she is pure feminine power—all circles, curves, extremes, and sensuality—and contrasts quite beautifully with IV, the Emperor. Her hands indicate the root of her power. Her right hand rests on her belly, showing us that everything she creates is part of her and comes, often

painfully, from her very core. Her left hand holds the heat, flame, and spark of magic, a deep connection with the very being of the universe.

The appearance of the Empress promises abundance in your life. She heralds a time of creativity. You are encouraged to tap into this energy and use it to positive advantage in your life. However, there is something very important to keep in mind while considering the act of creation. Our Empress, our Mother Nature, may manifest ultimately as a calm pastoral scene, a charming field, or a lush garden, but these soul-restoring environments were built on endless births and deaths. The process isn't always pretty. A baby may be born, a painting may emerge on a canvas, or a story may be told. It all comes from the heart of your creative being; as it fights its way into this world, expect a little bit of a mess.

• • • •

Reading tip: The Empress is often associated not just with Mother Nature but also with mothers and motherhood in general. This card can indicate your own mother. It can also indicate pregnancy, especially if the Ace of Wands is also present.

IV, THE EMPEROR

• • • •

"Nature provides us with great bounty once a year. I make sure we have something to eat every day."

Core meaning: Creating order and stability.

The Emperor, unlike the Empress, has strictly political and worldly associations. Like the Empress, this card reflects the ideal characteristics of the role. As we have seen, the Empress is the essence of creative power, which is based on ever-changing cycles. The Emperor, on the other hand, generates straight lines, grids, and constancy. Associated with the number four, the Emperor embodies all the characteristics of that number, including stability and reliability.

Through creating plans and systems, he ensures the effective distribution of resources, ideally providing enough for all. The four emblems on his throne represent the four elements of air, water, earth, and fire. Symbolically, these are the finite resources at his disposal that must be used for the good of all. Through creating systems upon which we depend, he creates peace and stability in daily life. In such an environment, we needn't worry constantly about basic survival. Instead, we have the safety and confidence needed to pursue other interests, such as art, philosophy, philanthropy, and spirituality. Sociologists who study ancient civilizations say that the ability of societies to create enough wealth to sustain their population with some margin of security coincides with the rise of spiritual and religious leaders within those societies. Security in terms of basic human needs is necessary for growth and enlightenment. Structures are meant to be foundations from which to fly. Unfortunately, in their negative extreme, these structures can become boxes or prisons that stifle individual expression.

When this card shows up in your reading, you know it is time to play the Emperor in your own life. Look for ways that you can create structures and systems to help organize and improve your situation. If you cannot, take enough responsibility to look for an authority figure that can assist or advise you. Consider your own sense of authority and responsibility and your relationships with others who have authority over or responsibility toward you. Are you fighting against or working within a healthy structure? Are you hiding within or ignoring a confining rules system?

• • • •

Reading tip: The number four carries a strong symbolic punch. The line separating the positive and negative aspects of the four can be a thin one. Watch for other fours showing up along with the Emperor. The Four of Cups and Four of Pentacles would skew the meaning toward a more stagnant and stifling energy. The Four of Wands and Four of Swords help lighten the natural solidness of the Emperor. The Emperor is also associated with fathers, fatherhood, and authority figures.

V, THE HIEROPHANT

. . . .

"Your every thought, word, and action expresses the truth of your soul."

Core meaning: Living faith in everyday life.

The name of this card comes from the word *hierophany* and means "the manifestation of the sacred." Consequently, the Hierophant is one who teaches us how to live in accordance with our sacred beliefs. For those belonging to a group, community, or organized religion, there are usually teachers aplenty. For those who follow a more solitary path, they are often their own hierophant. This responsibility is often supplemented by studying sacred texts, works of art, private spiritual practices, and nature.

This card has not always been called the Hierophant. In the oldest of decks it was titled the Pope, also known as the Pontiff, which means "bridge." He is the bridge between theory and practice. He creates a connection between spiritual belief and daily life. In this image he sits between a pile of books, representing the culmination of human spiritual understanding, and a tree, representing, for example, a living practice and the inherent knowledge of good and evil. Both the books and the tree represent roots and tradition, wisdom gained through the ages. The apple, such a mundane symbol, brings to mind many things. Students used to give apples to their teachers. Although not technically correct, many people say that Eve gave Adam an apple, leading

to their self-consciousness and banishment from Paradise. If you cut an apple crosswise, the center forms a pentagram, representing the four elements of the physical world under the guidance of Spirit. Our Hierophant, shown here as a humble, compassionate, and wise teacher, weaves together all these notions and more, and gives them to us as keys to open up our own understanding. With all teachings, it is up to individuals to take them into their heart and mind and to ultimately decide whether or not to envelop them into their life.

When the Hierophant comes to your reading, the most important thing to ask yourself is how what you believe matches what you think, say, and do. This card can represent a teacher who will help you identify your beliefs and assist you in determining how to best express those beliefs in your life.

• • • •

Reading tip: The Hierophant is often connected with traditional religion and religious leadership, and therefore can represent marriage, especially with the Four of Wands, the Lovers, and the Two, Nine, or Ten of Cups. This card also indicates starting a formal training or educational program, such as pursuing a university degree or certification program of any sort. If other surrounding cards are negative or repressive, such as the Devil, the Moon, the Five or Seven of Swords, or the Four of Pentacles, there may be a misuse of power, deception, or spiritual manipulation present in the situation.

VI, THE LOVERS

• • • •

"I could not have made a better choice."

Core meaning: Making a decision
that makes your heart glad.

Love is an interesting phenomenon, and this is an interesting card. In our everyday lives and in most readings about relationships, if the Lovers comes up, we cannot help but get a little giddy and excited about the possibilities. This card conjures up romantic hopes and dreams of, as Sally Owens said in *Practical Magic*, "A love that even time will lie down and be still for." There is something about the power of love that lets us believe that anything is possible, if only we were with the right person.

Why do we feel that way? Because when the right two things (or people) are mixed together, the newly created whole is worth more (or is better) than the sum of its parts. Put the right two people together and they both become their very best selves. In this image, a man, representing fire and air (the active elements), and a woman, representing water and earth (the passive elements), join hands. Their union creates something more astonishing and more powerful than they would ever be as individuals.

The experience of romantic love, while a very real force in our lives, is also symbolic of a deeper truth. It reminds us that whenever the two right things come together, something transformative and magical happens. These two things can be you plus any other thing you choose—a relationship, a career, a passion, anything—that is the perfect match for your heart. Really, this is the crux of this card: the importance of making the right choice. Make the right decision and the experience is full of the same potent power of love.

When the Lovers come a'calling, pay attention to your heart. You have the opportunity to make a choice—to commit to something that could change your life. This partnership has the potential for real magic. You've heard the saying "My heart just isn't in it"? If you are considering something (or someone!) and your heart doesn't leap at the thought, you might want to move on to the next thought.

• • • •

Reading tip: If the Two or Ten of Cups or the Four of Wands is present with this card, it is a good signal that romance or romantic love is playing a role in situation.

VII, THE CHARIOT

• • • •

**"Despite any concerns you may have,
I am in control of this situation."**

Core meaning: The triumph of will
in difficult circumstances.

The thunder of hoofbeats shakes the earth and yet her slight form remains perfectly still as the horsepower vibrates the reins. This confident young woman is intent upon forward movement and progress in the face of many challenges. The energy she directs is moving at dangerously high speeds. In the midst of the swirling chaos, she remains steady and focused.

The beasts powering her vehicle are opposites of each other, representing opposing forces that make the situation so challenging. Under normal circumstances, these energies want to move in different directions. Luckily, she has mastered the lessons of the Magician, the High Priestess, the Empress and Emperor, the Hierophant, and the Lovers and is ready to make her mark in the world.

In other tarot decks, the charioteer is shown holding a wand, a symbol of his will and of the force that guides the energies present toward his desired goal. In Elizabeth Peters's Amelia Peabody series (in which a Victorian archeologist couple explores Egypt), the main character carries a parasol that doubles as a weapon. In the steampunk mysteries by Gail Carriger, the Parasol Protectorate series, the

heroine, Alexia Tarabotti, carries a steampunked parasol modified with amazing gadgets and technologies, making it a useful weapon. In both books, the women use the parasols to promote action on behalf of their wills. Hence, our powerful Charioteer carries on this proud literary tradition and pays homage to Amelia Peabody and Alexia Tarabotti. Her parasol is also a symbol of power, will, and ingenuity.

If it is your turn to drive the chariot, you will find yourself wanting to move in a certain direction. You will be confident in that decision. Getting started will be the hardest part. Things are going to conspire against you, or so it will seem. Yet you have the skills and knowledge necessary to harness those contrary energies and head them in the right direction. Once you are moving, there won't be much that can stop you until you reach your goal.

VIII, STRENGTH

. . . .

**"Thank you for your kind aid. Instead
of devouring you, I will serve you."**

Core meaning: Calm control and
healing that brings strength.

Respectful Victorians exhibited their own unique form of
strength by keeping a stiff upper lip and repressing—er,
controlling—their base, or animal, instincts and desires. In
this card, we add a healthy dose of the "punk" from our
theme of "steampunk." In our version of Strength, a gentle
woman performs a revolutionary (or so it would seem to a
Victorian) act of strength.

Cards from older tarot decks show a human wrestling a
wild lion. This expressed the idea that people had a wild,
or evil, side of themselves that must be constantly fought,
repressed, and controlled or it would take them over and
utterly destroy them.

This woman suggests a different tack. She believes the
lion that stalks her is simply a symbol of her shadow self. In
Jungian terms, the shadow self is comprised of all the parts
of ourselves that we dislike, don't value, and are ashamed
of. These parts, she says, are not bad in and of themselves; rather, they are aspects of ourselves that have been
wounded. If ignored or repressed, they become infected.
After a while, they grow so large that they burst...showing

up in our lives in inappropriate and even destructive ways. This approach, she insists, never works in the long run.

Instead, she counsels that we approach our inner monsters with compassion, because that makes it easier to determine what caused the damage in the first place. Once we identify that root cause, we can remove it, just as she has extracted that gear from her lion's paw. Yes, it hurts, and yes, it is scary. The lion will probably roar—you may even get scratched or bitten. But it must be done, for only then can healing begin. From this healing comes strength.

Just as in the fable of the mouse who pulled the thorn from the lion's paw, after the hard part is over, the lion will be a devoted servant. In the same way, our shadow selves, grateful and healed, can be integrated into our whole personality. What we hid from—our anger, our fear, our emotional needs—we now welcome and learn how to express in our lives in a healthy and useful manner.

When confronted with the Strength card, you are well advised to tap into your deepest inner strength and express it with calm compassion. The infinity symbol in the Magician represents your connection with the energy of the universe; in this card it represents your connection with all aspects of yourself. In the Magician, this connection generates extraordinary power. In this card, it creates amazing strength. Find that connection; feel that strength. Do not forget to apply it with a light touch. A little goes a long way.

IX, THE HERMIT

• • • •

*"To see the glow of your own
light, go into the dark."*

Core meaning: Retreating from distractions
to determine your own truth.

In the great city that was Victorian London, communication was easier than at any other time in human history. Information was shared quickly, and there was plenty of it. People were making progress in all areas. Knowledge abounded. Naturally, when one is the recipient of so much data, it is easy to assume that a lot of input equals increased wisdom. Upon reflection, we know that simply is not true. In addition, in the midst of so much intellectual noise, there is the danger of one's own true voice being drowned.

The lights from a city mask the stars from our sight. In order to see them clearly, we move away from the civilized world. The Hermit knows that it is necessary from time to time to leave the din of society. Only in quiet solitude can he hear the voice of his heart. Only in the darkness can he see his own light.

He stands on what looks like a reechy junk pile. This represents the information, ideas, and philosophies he has collected on his journey. Some of it he discards; it does not resonate with his soul. Some of the more valuable pieces are added to his belief system. All of it, though, creates the framework from which he can view the world. All of it, whether rejected or adopted, in some way adds to his truth.

When the Hermit visits you, he heralds a time of solitude. There are times when it is worth seeking out the opinions of others, but this is not one of them. There are times when you need to ignore those opinions and decide for yourself what is right and true. Retreat from the maddening crowd. In the quiet and in the dark, you will be able to see your answers shining brightly. Once you see it, hold it high and be guided by it.

• • • •

Reading tip: If this card shows up in a reading about romance, it usually indicates being single for a time. It is likely there are important lessons to be learned before being ready for a relationship. The surrounding cards should give a clue about what those lessons are.

X, THE WHEEL OF FORTUNE

"The dice are rattling. Snake eyes or lucky seven? Ah, that is the question. It is always the question."

Core meaning: A random occurrence is at hand.

We do love our clockworks and gears—machines that do what we want and that measure the moments of our lives. Punctuality, we all know, is the sign of a civilized people. It is only by everyone agreeing to a specific reality, such as what time it is, that allows us to run the trains and keep the engines of society moving forward. It is only natural, isn't it? The stars move with constant regularity across the night's sky. The seasons follow one another in strict procession. The stuff of life, the elemental energies of the universe, all abide by the rules of their nature. With sufficient data, there is no reason why we cannot predict anything with absolute precision.

That is the great lure of systems and order, of knowledge and so-called progress. Knowing what is going to happen gives us false confidence. We are not facing the day with such assuredness because we are certain of the rightness of our actions or the clarity of our connection with the Divine. We feel safe because we know what will happen; we will not be surprised.

The stars do move according their orbits. The cycle of life does repeat itself. The laws of the universe do govern our physical world. Perhaps that last statement is not quite as absolute, but it has been working for us fairly well. And yet, for some reason, things do not always play out as reason and the natural order of things would suggest, and we come to the cards because we don't feel certain about our future. There are three reasons we don't know. The first is because we lack important data and therefore cannot make an accurate prediction. Tarot can help with this, of course. The second is because the future is not yet fully determined. Tarot can let us know how and to what extent we can shape the still-nebulous future. The third is because there are elements at play that are, O horror of horrors, completely random.

Yes, it is as if someone is playing dice with your life. Something will happen that makes no sense or could not have been foreseen.

The Wheel of Fortune represents the random hand of fate, which can be lucky or unlucky. There is no judgment or assessment of your life in this card; it is more impersonal than Justice or the Tower, for example. Randomness is as much a part of life as the natural order. This card gives you a heads-up that something unexpected is about to drop into your life.

• • • •

Reading tip: This card is indeed a heads-up—we could say a warning, but that implies something "bad" or "unlucky," and the Wheel can bring "good" and "lucky" events as well. It tells you to take notice. You can glean a bit more of the direction of the Wheel by the surrounding cards and the question. Cards that suggest a happy situation suggest that things will change for the better even if there is no logical reason to think so, and vice versa. The Wheel with the Ace of Pentacles is often a very lucky combination.

XI, JUSTICE

• • • •

**"You play the hand that you were
dealt. The way you play it will
determine your next hand."**

Core meaning: The consequences
of your actions are at hand.

Her gaze looks right through you, into the very core of
your soul, shining a light on your motivations and intents.
Stones and gems and crystals, tokens of your actions, fill
one side of the scale. A feather floats gently to the other, the
weight of a pure heart and a clean soul. Compared to our
earthy humanness, how can the scales ever balance?

Karmic justice is a complex matter. The equation com-
paring stones and feathers is a delicate balance. This is no
simple operation. She must take into account every past
experience, every thought and hope and fear, all your darkness and all your light, and mix it with the lessons your soul
has determined to learn in this lifetime. So many variables
could create a cluttered, indecipherable mess, but her scales
are precise and her objectivity complete. The end result, the
final judgment, is the perfect result of your own decisions.
The cards that fall from her hand are the ones you selected.

When Justice appears in your reading, it is a reminder
that your actions have created your present situation. If
you are not happy with the current state of things, examine
your intentions, motivations, and decisions with the clear

and objective eyes of Justice. Measure your actions against your ideal. The notion that your present actions create your future is always true. It is an ongoing cycle. But if this card shows up, it is letting you know that now is a pivotal time. Whatever you are considering doing in this situation has greater ramifications than you may have realized.

If you are feeling that something in your life "isn't fair," this card will be a gentle reminder that you should look within before blaming others or fickle fate for your current challenges.

Likewise, if you are worried that someone else is getting away with something and you want to insure that they "pay for their crimes," the Justice cards lets you know that you don't need to worry. The universe has it under control and does not need your help at this time. You have enough on your plate keeping your own karma in order.

• • • •

Reading tip: If the reading involves questions of legal decisions, this card lets you know that a fair judgment will come. Whether that judgment is in your favor, though, is not guaranteed.

XII, THE HANGED MAN

· · · ·

**"A little shift in perception,
that's all that was needed."**

Core meaning: Willing surrender
to an experience or situation.

The Victorian era has a reputation for preferring strict control of all things at all times. And really, we modern humans also prefer order to chaos. Knowing what is expected of us and what to expect from our environment allows us to feel secure. We don't need to worry about our general safety and can get on with other, more important things.

Inventors, creators, and anyone who has ever had a brilliant idea know that being safe is not always conducive to flashes of genius. Sometimes we need to be turned on our head, figuratively or even literally, rather like our Hanged Man here. If you turn this card upside down, you notice his legs create the number 4, a symbol of stability, security, and safety...and also, in its extreme incarnation, of stagnation. Our man has been turned upside down, allowing him to see things from a completely different point of view. The stagnant and uninspired state has been shaken.

Allowing himself to be put in this position is a sacrifice of his dignity, his safety, and his worldview. This posture, with his feet above his head, represents a temporary override of the mind and its analytical approach. The striving for order and rationality is put on hiatus. While the head

is associated with logic, feet correspond to our connection with the earth. The elevation of his feet represents placing higher value on his connection to nature. For a time, he is experiencing the world differently than is his wont. He must remain so long enough to relax, long enough for vines to nutate around his wrists and for nature to cover his chains. In return for his sacrifices, he gains illumination, a moment of intense brightness when everything, at least for a moment, falls into perfect place.

If the Hanged Man pays a visit to your reading, prepare yourself for some sort of epiphany. But first, expect an uncomfortable time. Let go of your safety nets, sacrifice your worldview, and trust the universe. You cannot rush this experience, so you may as well settle down and just take a look around. No doubt things will look different from here; enjoy the view.

• • • •

Reading tip: Traditionally the Hanged Man represents sacrifice and martyrdom. This can be brought to a negative extreme if the Ten of Swords is present in the reading. The card has also, in the oldest of decks, symbolized a traitor, which could be the case if the Five or Seven of Swords is present.

XIII, DEATH

••••

**"The gentle silence of Death takes
all your sorrow, transforms it, and
gives it back to you as love."**

Core meaning: An ending making
transformation possible.

The Victorians did death right, with drama and flair. This is
something we modern folks have lost. We clean it up, put it
in special buildings, attend the service, and quickly get on
with life. This shift is reflected in modern tarot interpretations of the card, where the focus is on new beginnings.

It is true that the Death card rarely predicts physical death (only once in my over twenty years of reading),
although if you think about it, it is the one prediction that
will always, at some point, come true. Everybody dies. In
tarot, though, it symbolizes the final end of something. It is
not sudden, as we see in the Tower card, but is an organic
conclusion, something that we have probably already felt
was nearing its end in our life. Divorce, loss of a job, ending
of a friendship, a rejection of a formerly followed spiritual
path…all these experiences are common in our lives or the
lives of our friends and loved ones. If we are honest, we
usually feel it coming. This card lets us know that what we
expected is nigh.

Even expected endings bring sadness. Mourning is natural and healthy. There is beauty and healing within it that is

necessary before moving on to whatever new relationships, events, or adventures await. When the shadow of Death crosses your threshold, look into her eyes. Make room for her in your life and in your heart. Connect with her. Feel her compassion and understanding. Accept that she is a natural part of the life cycle. Allow her silence to wash over you, absorb your pain, and heal you. Pay your respects. Hold the memory within. All you experience is part of you; bring all of yourself forward as you move on.

XIV, TEMPERANCE

• • • •

**"The difference between a
professional and an amateur is that
a professional makes it look easy."**

Core meaning: The right thing at
the right time in the right place.

Most people look at her and see a rather plain woman,
bland and, at first glance, unremarkable. A bit strange, what
with the bare feet and bizarre water juggling. What they
probably don't see are the powerful red wings. People see
what they want to see, after all. Surely this odd creature
isn't some spiritually evolved being. Yes, she has that eso-
teric symbol on her corset, but really, everyone is wearing
those these days. It doesn't mean anything…does it?

Most people would be mistaken. But you aren't, are you?
I didn't think so.

Temperance is nothing more and nothing less than perfection. Perfection, like "truth," is not an absolute. It var-
ies according to the situation and the moment. People
sometimes think that one "attains" perfection. The state of
perfection is not static; one does not so much achieve it as
maintain it. Being perfect is to be in constant motion, for
you must adjust to the ever-changing currents of life in a
perpetual balancing act. The key to this is being sensitive
to the energy of the universe. The more aware you are of
everything that is going on around you and the better you

understand how energy flows and reacts, the easier it is to move through life with grace.

Look at our plain girl again. She is, first and foremost, fully herself, completely in her body, centered and calm. One foot is on the earth, and one is in the water. She levitates disks in the air. She wears the sign of fire. She is connected and in tune with the elements. She is winged, and her crown chakra is illuminated. Although grounded, she also maintains a clear connection with the Divine. Because of all of this, she is perfectly poised to be in the right place at the right time and is almost guaranteed to do the right thing.

When you get this card in a reading, what does all this mean for you? First of all, calm down. This is a card of peace and grace. Do not court chaos; do not invite confusion. Be quietly aware of everything around you. Everything you need to know is present. Feel it. React appropriately. Temperance is more complex than "moderation." It is more like Buddhism's Noble Eightfold Path and its emphasis on "right." That version of "right" is not black and white. Some may think that makes it harder to grasp, but it doesn't—not really. If you are aware and listen, you know what is right.

• • • •

Life tip: Temperance is the center of the Wheel of Fortune. If you don't want to be tossed about by the randomness of life, make Temperance your goal. Then, whatever happens, you are in perfect control of yourself rather than being controlled by events.

XV, THE DEVIL

· · · ·

"It's bloody hard work keeping this thing going."

Core meaning: A choice, situation, or action
that is contrary to your best interest.

Literature and movies are peppered with stories of the
creations of man going awry. These machines, these monsters, these situations all began as a great idea that became
a viable plan and eventually manifested in the physical
world. Because we have already invested so much into these
blessed creations of ours, we carefully nurture them. They
are fed and praised and loved. Our lives are rearranged to
make room for them, to make it easier for them to grow
larger and stronger. It happens so slowly, so naturally, that
we don't realize what we've actually brought to life.

By the time our creation has fully matured, we've completely assimilated its care and feeding into our lives. We
cannot imagine what we'd do without it. We are it, and it is
us; there is no division. We can't imagine ever being completely free of it, and in truth, we really don't want to be.
To separate from it will surely mean death. But this really
doesn't matter, in any case; we are too busy taking care of
this thing to think about such nonsense.

If the Devil is part of your life (and if he shows up in
a reading, then he is indeed part of your life), take a look
at what you've created that has taken over your life, your

resources, your energy, and your focus. More importantly, what have you nurtured that is completely connected to your self-identity? This card represents your commitment to something that is so all-consuming that you cannot imagine your life without it. But this thing—even if it started life innocently and with the very best of intentions—now exists merely to be constantly fed. It gives nothing of use in return. It only consumes: your resources…your life…you.

As hideous as that may seem, there is a bright side. Because you created this life-ingesting monster machine, you can dismantle it. Also, once you've finished that, you get to decide where you want to invest all the time and energy you'll have on hand.

• • • •

Reading tip: In traditional decks, the Devil is a perversion of the Lovers and of the Hierophant, both compositionally and literally. Therefore, it symbolizes doing something that goes against one's spiritual beliefs and doing something against one's greatest good. Because of this, when the Devil shows up, it has a tendency to twist or skew cards toward their more negative extremes. This card can also appear in situations involving addictions.

XVI, THE TOWER

• • • •

"If it doesn't kill you,
it makes you stronger."

Core meaning: An unexpected
event that changes everything.

Let's just say it plainly: people hardly ever want to see the
Tower card in their reading.

At the end of the day, this is a card that indicates the
destruction of something. Generally speaking, that something has been carefully created and nurtured. It has value;
it is something we love. It is, in fact, intrinsic to our worldview and our life.

Like the tree city in the image, this ornate and complex
structure began humbly enough, with roots deep within the
earth, connecting us with the very essence that feeds our
being. As it grew, it became less organic and more complicated. Artifice became more important than substance. It is
a thing of beauty and mostly functional and useful.

Then destruction comes, raining down from the very
heavens, and your structure is crushed. You didn't desire
this. But you've been alive long enough to know that things
like this do happen in our lives.

The Tower card is not merely a portent of destruction. As
with all the cards, there is a lesson. Change happens in all
our lives; in fact, life *is* change. We've seen different kinds

of change in the Wheel and in Death. They had their lessons, and the Tower has its own wisdom.

We build structures in our lives—worldviews, philosophies, spiritual practices, and lifestyles. Structures are meant to enhance our lives, to give us just enough security so that we can soar. When the structure overtakes our spirit, that structure is no longer serving a beneficial purpose. The thing we created to enhance our life is now destroying it. The natural reaction of the universe, then, is to destroy that structure in order to save our life.

When the Tower blasts its way into your life, batten down the hatches and prepare for a rough time. The real work begins after the crash. Look at what was destroyed, and let it go. More importantly, look at what remains. It has survived a trial by fire; make sure you recognize its value. Pick it up and plan on fitting it into your new structure. This is the universe's idea of repurposing.

XVII, THE STAR

• • • •

"Huʃ, my darling, ɧuʃ. Have faiʈ. I will ligɧt your way."

Core meaning: Guidance, serenity, and hope.

A little note before diving into the beautiful depths of this card: the whole "fate" and "destiny" discussion is fraught with strong opinions and emotions. First, we have the question of whether the future, any of it, is in any way predetermined or even knowable. If it is not, then consulting the cards for information on the future loses some of its usefulness. Second, some tarotists spend many happy hours debating the definitions, similarities, and differences between the words *fate* and *destiny*. Because the ideas of fate and destiny are interwoven in the various meanings of this particular card, it helps for each reader to be clear on his or her beliefs and adapt the possible interpretations accordingly.

From her flowing skirts mingling with the turbulent, confusing waves of the ocean to the shining clarity in the palm of her hand, the Star is a lifeline. First and foremost, she calms the heart and mind with the reassurance that all will be well. She wordlessly invites you to drink in her peace and serenity. Breathe deeply and slowly. Gaze upon the vastness of the starry, starry sky and gain perspective. Know that the universe is in fine working order. Only when you settle down can you see and receive her gifts.

Once settled, accept her offerings. What does she offer you? As the Star, she can give many things. Starlight, star bright...make a wish. She is a kind goddess whom you can petition; requests to her are often granted. "All I ask is a tall ship and a star to steer her by." From the three wise men of ancient lore to intrepid starship captains, a star is a source of guidance. Back in the Fool card and again in the Hermit we saw this light, this guiding force that is within our soul and resonating with the Divine. We sometimes have difficulty seeing or sensing it. In our darkest hours, we know it as the brightest star in the sky, a message of grace and a lifeline to gently lead us back on course.

And what of star-crossed lovers and the like? Ah, here is the tricky issue of fate and destiny! Are we fated to love a specific person? Are we destined to play a certain role? Does this card mark that? Possibly. Remember, though, she is a harbinger of peace and healing. If the notion comforts you and helps you follow your soul's true light, then why could she not?

When you see the Star, you can relax! You came to a reading looking for guidance, and it shall be given to you. Our Star sits on an astrolabe, an ancient computing device used to determine the positions of celestial bodies in the night sky. She knows where you are as well as where you are going and can help you see the way. She rises above the troubled waters of your soul and gives you a light to follow when you cannot find it within yourself.

XVIII, THE MOON

• • • •

"It was all so strange, and I cannot remember it properly. Well, you know how dreams can be."

Core meaning: A situation of flux and uncertainty, fraught either with deception or the revealing of important truths.

Suddenly—or slowly (you are not really sure at this point; everything is so blurry)—you are on the edge of an ocean in the dark. You sense rather than see the presence of creatures of some sort. Sounds of softly disturbed water, as loud as thunder in the silence, set you on edge. That edge is sharpened as whirring, creaking mechanical noises add to the harmony. Your eyes adjust to the darkness just as two pillars that you didn't know were there come to life, moving, turning, adjusting…and finally clicking, a surprisingly gentle sound. The clouds part, the cold orb overhead glows, and your world is caressed by illumination. You squint. You shiver. Confusion, curiosity, and the tiniest tremor of terror travel through your veins.

While our conscious selves are busy building things that may become our own personal devils, our subconscious selves are also busy creating. The activities of the subconscious help us assimilate the experiences of our lives into our worldview, solve problems, and heal emotional wounds

via dreams, intuitive and psychic flashes, and communication with the Divine. As with all things, the realm of the subconscious has its dark side. In tarot, this realm is revealed, in a manner of speaking, in the Moon card. While the High Priestess sometimes communicates with dreams, the Moon's language is nightmares. The High Priestess lifts the veils on mysteries; the Moon sprinkles confusion. The High Priestess's gift is, ultimately, wisdom. The Moon…is much more complicated.

Oh, the irony of attempting to speak of the Moon with clarity. The Moon represents the kind of darkness that promises hidden treasures where there are really dangers and alerts you to monsters when none are present. It shows everything as other than it is. On a mundane level, it warns you that things are not as they seem, that you should take nothing at face value, that you must question everything, and that you should consider waiting until morning (metaphorically speaking) before deciding your next move. You really don't have all the facts and could take a misstep—or not. Who knows? It's best to just sit on the riverbank, pet the cat, and see what secrets are revealed.

On another level, the Moon is a place of inspiration and imagination. You can see and experience things you've never dreamt of before. Feed your creativity and seek your muse in this shadowland. Confront your demons and battle your dragons. Achieve inexplicable victories against the monsters of your mind. Find freedom. Become paralyzed with fear, sink below the water's surface, lose yourself to your worst nightmares. It is a dangerous place. When confronting the Moon on this level, it might be comforting to remember that, as Yoda said, the only things you'll find here are those you bring with you.

• • • •

Reading tip: The Moon is a tricky card. So much of its interpretation will depend upon the question and the surrounding cards. If the High Priestess is also present, focus more on internal intuitive work or experiences. If the Devil card is present (or other cards that lend an unpleasant feel to the reading, such as the Seven of Wands or perhaps the Three of Swords), turn to a more mundane approach; it is possible that someone is keeping secrets or withholding information. It is easy to assume that other people are lying, but it is just as easy and perhaps even more common to lie to oneself.

XIX, THE SUN

· · · ·

"Dance with me."

"Why?"

"Because life is amazing."

Core meaning: Clarity that brings joy.

Tarot authors share some qualities with Victorian writers...the tendency toward verbosity being one of them. That trait, coupled with the demands of book construction and editors, both of which value consistency, means that we authors tend to say more about this card than is absolutely necessary. After all, if we only wrote a few lines for the Sun—compared to several paragraphs for the other cards—it wouldn't be fair to the Sun, and, worse, it would be inconsistent.

But the truth is that the Sun is a very simple card. The sun symbolizes solar wisdom, a conscious understanding. We all know that knowing something can be either good or bad; that knowledge can make us either happy or unhappy (or some other emotion). There is a reason they say, for example, "The truth hurts" and "If you don't want to know, don't ask." The knowledge of the Sun card, though, is joyful.

If you've ever just felt so happy that laughter bubbled out of you, then you've experienced the Sun. In those moments, it seems like there is no real reason for such happiness—but there is. When I said the Sun was a simple card, perhaps

I should have said that the *experience* of it is very simple; the reasons are complex. What happens is that everything in the universe lines up perfectly, and you experience this moment of crystalline clarity. You are connected in a million different indefinable ways to the universe, and it feels amazing. We see this interconnectedness in the card: the male and female elements are dancing together; the rational self (the sun) and the intuitive self/soul (the dog) are both present and shining; the creations of man (wall) and nature (sunflowers) exist in harmony. Everything is, at least for this brief moment, utterly and completely perfect.

When this card shines in your life, it promises happiness and joy based on truth and understanding. Its presence uplifts all other cards and makes everything just a little bit better.

• • • •

Reading tip: If you are looking for a yes or a no as part of your reading, the Sun, as well as the aces, are usually read as clear yeses. The Sun card can also represent a full year if you are looking for timing, and it is associated with birthdays (which are referred to in astrological circles as your solar return).

XX, JUDGEMENT

• • • •

"When the music beats to the
rhythm of your heart and echoes
the melody of your soul, you can
only ignore it for so long."

Core meaning: Hearing and heeding a call.

Dwelling in the aether betwixt heaven and earth, the duti-
ful angel turns the handle...and the music plays. You know
that saying "March to the beat of your own drummer"?
She inspired it—only she plays a gramophone, not a drum.
The strange mystery of it all is that she is playing the same
record and yet everyone hears a different tune.

The story of the beautiful, solemn gramophone player
in the aether is, sadly, not real. Like so much else, she is
a metaphor. To make things even more confusing, she is
not a metaphor for Judgement, as the name of the card
implies. We would do better to call this one something else,
like Resurrection, Renaissance, Revivification, Renewal, or
Rebirth, perhaps. In some ways, she is Rescue. In any case,
she plays the music of the heavens that can only be heard
by your soul. When your soul hears it and if it can get your
conscious mind (which can be very stubborn) to listen, the
message usually changes your life. Actually, to be more precise, the message will save your life. You are granted the
gift of the aetheric angelic music when you are in danger of

dying—not a physical death but a spiritual one. Your life is not going in the right direction, and it is time to shift gears.

More than likely, whatever you are being asked to do will scare the bejeebies out of you. Try not to give in to fear, because even though it is radical, this change, it is what you are meant to do, what you were born to do. Rising from the quiet numbness of the tomb is always a little jarring, but once you embrace the music and breathe deeply, you will wonder how you could bear that old life for so long.

Here's the secret of this card: you already know what you are supposed to do. If you are honest with yourself, it will be very clear. When this card calls to you in a reading, it is a clear sign that yes, you *should* do whatever it is that you have been thinking of doing.

XXI, THE WORLD

• • • •

"Ta-da!"

Core meaning: Successful completion.

If the World shows up in your reading, stand up and take a bow! Excellent job. You should be proud of yourself!

As the final card in the Major Arcana, the World marks the end of a journey. There are plenty of cards in tarot that mark endings: all of the tens, Death, and the Tower, for example. All of these endings have different flavors. The flavor of the World is successful completion. It is not merely a situation playing itself out, as described by the tens, or the natural or unexpected experiences of Death or the Tower. It is a finishing of something that you started, that you wanted, and that you worked toward.

The woman in this card, often referred to as the World Dancer, is the essence of ease and comfort, surrounded as she is by symbols of the elements—air, water, fire, and earth—as well as the large gear, or "world," representing everything that is. She moves gracefully in this environment, confident that she has mastered everything she needed and wanted to. As with all endings, there is also a bittersweet flavor, because one cannot rest long on one's laurels. With this wonderful achievement, she is now ready to move on to the next cycle—and so are you. Congratulations and bon voyage!

. . . .

Reading tip: The World, like the Sun and the aces, indicates a yes if you are looking for one. It also suggests travel—particularly long distance, especially if the Chariot or a knight is present, or more local travel if the Six of Swords shows up.

Chapter 3

MINOR ARCANA

ACE OF WANDS

• • • •

**"Forget the big bang—I can create
a universe with this tiny spark."**

Core meaning: An opportunity to
harness and express your will.

Boldness, courage, and determination characterize the suit
of wands. As you journey through this suit you will see the
stories of human passion and will. In the suit of cups, we
will see our relationships; in swords, our thoughts; and in
pentacles, our physical experience. In this suit, we are taking action, expending energy, and creating. Throughout our
lives we will celebrate, decide, defend, and explore. These
activities are initiated and carried out by our will. At its

core, this suit is the exploration of will—of our raw strength in its many human forms.

Wands are associated with fire, and fire is, like all good symbols, complex. At its best, it gives light and life to the world. At its worst, it utterly destroys, growing stronger as it consumes. This power within each of us has the ability to create or demolish, depending on what we use it for. Fire burns within us not only as will and strength but also as passion. A close cousin to passion is creativity, also associated with fire and the suit of wands. As a fire rages through a forest, it destroys, but it also purifies. Because of this quality, wands are also connected with spirituality.

The lively energy of wands and fire leads us to expect action and lots of it. Ironically, the cards in this suit are just as much about stillness as about motion. Underneath all the exciting words that express the wands—such as boldness, passion, energy, and creation—is will. As a rule, I detest books that quote the dictionary, and I have never done so. However, as a lover of dictionaries and etymology, I am making an exception here to talk more about the word *will*. (Besides, I am consulting a Victorian-era dictionary, which therefore fits the theme.) My 1891 *Webster's* talks about the word's Latin roots: To determine; to decide in the mind that something shall be done or forborne, implying power to carry the purpose into effect, and also to set or to stretch forward. The will is a faculty of the mind. It happens internally. What it decides affects future events. As you read the descriptions of the Two, Three, Seven, and Nine of Wands, keep this aspect of the will—its function and its power—in mind. It is a deceptively quiet activity but oh-so-very potent.

The Ace of Wands exudes power but also the complexity of the suit at its most positive. The metal of the hand and wand are strengthened and purified by fire and thus made worthy. The surrounding candles echo the sacred light shining behind the hand. The energy—the will—is unadulterated and ready to be put to use. The wand itself is a magnificent and clearly magical creation. The base is an ornate representation of human creativity. The gears represent human action and desire for progress. The wand miraculously becomes a living thing, symbolizing the connection between an action and its spiritual roots.

When the gift of the Ace of Wands graces your reading, realize it for the gift it is and prepare yourself to take that energy and make the most of it. Like all the aces, it represents a fleeting moment in time. If you don't take it and feed it, it will burn out, leaving only the ashes of regret behind. The Ace of Wands is a supercharged boost of energy that you can apply however you like. If you do take it, be clear about your intent, as it is your will more than anything that determines the direction that events will take. Yes, you have much power at your fingertips at the moment, and with that comes much responsibility.

TWO OF WANDS

• • • •

**"A wielder of fire does not chant
'eenie-meanie-miny-moe.'"**

Core meaning: Hesitating over a decision.

Morose and alone, he holds what he is certain is the greatest opportunity of his life. The power rests in his hands, growing weaker. Although he looks pitiful, few would pity him. Nay, they'd give a great deal to have his particular problem, for he has both resources and options; he can do as he pleases, and yet, at least for now, he does nothing. Let's hope he does something before paralyzing fear overtakes him entirely.

In the Ace of Wands we spoke of the fiery action and determination of the suit of wands. This card, however, is the exception to that rule. For here, in the moment of indecision, the element of fire is not happy. Having no firm direction or purpose, it will die. The number two suggests either decision or union; neither of these actions are being taken here.

The wandlike pillars represent two viable choices. Not only is he blessed with options, but he also has an excellent view of the big picture. Just looking at him, immobile, potentially wasting this opportunity, would make most people crazy. Some will shout, "Pick the red one!" Others will encourage, "The blue! The blue is best!"

Up there, removed from others, he won't hear. He faces his potential future alone, weighted by concern about picking the "right" one.

If you find yourself in such an enviable position as having the Two of Wands appear in your reading, take a lesson from this indecisive individual. Doing nothing is the worst choice. A dynamic, wands-charged situation requires action. Break the balance; end the stalemate. If you seek guidance in deciding, consider the connotations of this suit. What feels bold? What choice would make you feel courageous? What ignites your passion? What connects you to your spiritual roots? Answer these questions, and your decision will be easy.

THREE OF WANDS

• • • •

*"This is my credo: clarity of
vision, strength of will, and
unshakeable determination. And
yes, it is working for me."*

Core meaning: Active waiting.

The tight balance of his device mirrors the taut line connecting him to his ships. In the vista of his mind, he pulls, hand over calloused hand, a thick, rough rope toward him.

The ships are coming in, and he leaves nothing to chance. From the shore, he scans the horizon. As he gathers information, adjustments are made to the beacons created specifically for this job. The beacons are masterfully crafted tools, the perfect alchemy of will and logic, of nature and machine. By constantly adjusting his vision and his thinking, he is helping the beacons shine as brightly as possible, guiding the ship he wants directly to his port. This is not simply waiting for dreams to come true. This is active waiting, with *active* being the key word. The waiting part is only true insofar as the ship isn't actually there yet.

If there is any card in the deck that expresses the concepts of the Law of Attraction (as popularized by Rhonda Byrne's *The Secret*), this is it. This card holds a nearly palpable vibrating energy. We can sense his will, and we see that *X* certainly does mark the spot, the center of energy. At the crux of the three wands, his determination and focus

come together, creating an irresistible magnet, attracting precisely what he wants.

When the Three of Wands visits you in a reading, you can be sure that your efforts are nearly ready to pay off. If you are wondering where your ship is, this card lets you know that you should focus and increase the flame of your will to hurry your ship home. It takes tremendous energy to reel in a big fish.

FOUR OF WANDS

· · · ·

"If you don't have a good time, it's your own silly fault!"

Core meaning: Celebrating the culmination of events or the achieving of a goal.

The irrepressible energy of the wands is expressed with exuberant joy in this card. If any number could repress fire, it would be the four. Structure and stability do not seem like natural friends for such an energetic element. What we see here, though, is that the right sort of structure can let fire shine even brighter.

Today is a special day...because they have decided to make it special. They are carving out a moment in time and an area in space to create a celebration. Wands are erected, festooned with bright flowers and ribbons. Rich cloths cover the ground. Generous baskets of food spill over abundantly. The enthusiastic event planners don their most festive party garb. Everything bright and colorful and delicious and wonderful is brought together. The effect is one of undeniable joy. The energy created here promises to shower more goodness on the participants, for one of the hostesses finds a fortuitous card among the party items, clearly a good omen that a good time will be had by all.

If you get invited to this party, you have probably finished up a creative endeavor and are ready to celebrate your achievement. More than likely, the project will have been a group effort or involved with a group in some way. One of the charming old-fashioned interpretations for this card is "marriage," perhaps because the structure resembles the bowers used at Jewish weddings. A marriage, too, is a creative endeavor (all that wooing!) and a group-related celebration.

• • • •

Reading tip: If this card is in the company of the Lovers, the Hierophant, the Two of Cups, or the Ten of Cups, a wedding may be in the future. Also, if paired with the Justice card, it could mean a civil ceremony–type of marriage coupled with a celebratory party.

FIVE OF WANDS

• • • •

"A little friendly competition never hurt anyone, right?"

Core meaning: Conflict.

It did not begin as a battle; no, nothing as destructive as that. Indeed, the intent was to work together for a common goal. But people with distinct approaches to a matter tend to collide. Each has his or her methods (represented by their different wands) and are likely quite talented. Unfortunately, the styles do not work easily together and the strong personalities all vie to take leadership.

The chaotic energy found in the number five fans the enthusiasm of the wands into flames. Comparisons and opinions grow more heated. Suddenly, assertive people become aggressive. Verbal bandying turns physical. All constructive impetus seems lost, burned to a cinder in the ensuing melee.

The Five of Wands is the element of fire at its most unpredictable and therefore most dangerous. There are too many unknowns and chaotic variables to make rational decisions. If you find yourself in this situation, fight if you must, but if possible, pull out of the fray. The sooner the situation ceases to be fed, the sooner it can die down. Once the energy stabilizes, you can assess the situation and move ahead more rationally. In addition, by removing yourself from active participation and just observing the others,

you can learn a thing or two about their methods and motivations. Use that knowledge as you move forward to keep such a conflagration from starting all over again.

SIX OF WANDS

• • • •

"All hail the conquering hero!"

Core meaning: Recognition of achievement.

She felt so proud to be part of the event, standing tall and holding one of the victory wands high as he rode past. He looked so noble in his dress uniform, carrying the laurels with such dignity. *How can he look so humble after all he has achieved?* she wondered. *Does he not know that he has not achieved this merely for himself? Does he not realize that what he has done, he has done on behalf of us all? His glory is our glory!*

He rode through the crowd, reflective and subdued, fully aware of the responsibility he bore. He did not do this for himself. The fire, the courage—the determination—came from them. "This is your victory, not mine," he wanted to shout. "I did not do this alone."

Two points of view. Two truths that weave together to create one experience. There has been a victory, a great deed, a wondrous accomplishment. The doer of the deed, the hero of the hour, is publicly recognized as such. Heroes hardly ever exist in a vacuum, and consequently, everyone who has touched his life is part of the victory. In any society, heroes play a role. When we see them, we see the hero within and all that we could accomplish. They inspire us to be more than we are. When the public honors a hero, they also honor the potential within themselves.

If this victorious hero parades into your reading, prepare to be publicly recognized for an achievement. Or perhaps you'll be a part of the crowd. If so, acknowledge the accomplishment and realize that this strength, will, and determination is available to you as well. Tap into and use it, and soon you'll be riding in the place of honor.

SEVEN OF WANDS

• • • •

"What are you willing to die for?
What are you willing to kill for?"

Core meaning: Defensiveness.

There is no doubt whatsoever in her mind; she knows she is right. There are those who believe just as vehemently that she is wrong. Below her, the cacophony grows louder, more ugly. They continue to gather, increasing in number and in aggressiveness. She is surprised to see people who she thought she knew, who she thought understood her; it hurts her to feel the separation from their goodwill. Yet her heart never falters. Her determination is ignited to a contained, calm but deadly fury. Make no mistake: she will defend herself. She only hopes she doesn't have to cross the line from defending herself to destroying someone else in order to survive. These ethical stances can be so complicated.

The structure she stands on represents her worldview. Finely crafted, complex, every element carefully selected, it contains all her values. This is her character and the source of her strength. This is how she knows what is worth fighting for. This is what fuels the fire of her determination. This is her certainty.

If this card shows up in your reading, you are surely feeling defensive. What is your platform like? What are you defending? Are you sure it is worth the effort? How far are you willing to go to defend your beliefs? What are you absolutely certain of?

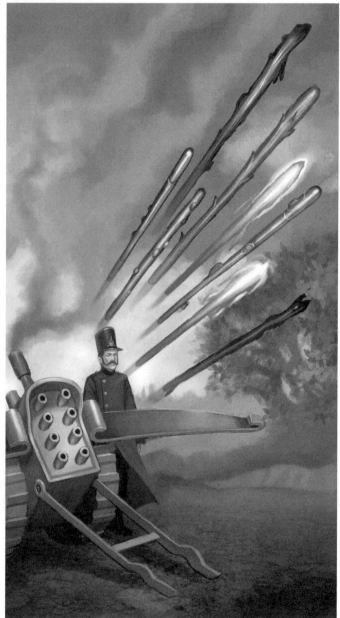

EIGHT OF WANDS

• • • •

"Once you press the 'fire' button, you can't unpress it."

Core meaning: Swift movement.

He has every confidence in this device. It has been precisely engineered by the nation's finest. It is meant to do one thing very, very well. Once released, the perfectly balanced wands go exactly where expected. Did he mention they'll do the job quickly as well? Speed is important, because a small window of time between initiating the procedure and its ultimate outcome lowers the possibility that something will interfere with the plan.

One small action from him—simply pulling a lever—sets in motion actions that have been in the works for years. *It is quite interesting,* he thinks, *that I am this tiny moment between all that came before and all that will come after. That's a bit of responsibility, really. Best not to think about it. If it weren't me working the lever, someone else would.*

The Eight of Wands is a fast-moving card of inevitability. Events that are currently in motion will quickly reach their resolution. They are situations that have been created over time, a series of actions and reactions that are now reaching their inexorable conclusion.

If you receive this card, you may feel very pleased if you have been making plans and hoping they will come together. This card is a positive signal that they will indeed unfold as you hope, and quite soon.

On the other hand, if you have had a feeling of unease, like something bad is about to occur, you won't be so happy to see this card. Even in this case, though, you have options if you are willing to take the consequences. That speedy, beautiful formation of wands can be turned to chaos fairly easily. The resulting mess might be worse, or it might not. Are you willing to risk it?

• • • •

Reading tip: A traditional meaning of this card is "receiving a message." Pages are also associated with messages. If a page shows up with the Eight of Wands, a message may play a key role in events. If you are waiting for news, this combination lets you know it will soon arrive.

NINE OF WANDS

• • • •

*"We'll have just enough time
to batten down the hatches
before the storm hits."*

Core meaning: Preparing for
the next challenge.

The precisely machined gears once ran so quietly that he had to rely on the gauges to know if the thing was running. Now, battered and in dire need of maintenance, it clangs and chugs, complaining loudly. *A lot like me,* he muses. "Damn knee hurts like a son of gun. Just as soon cut my head off than feel it pound one more time." He peers through the telescope. "No time for complaining; the next round is on the way. Best prioritize this disaster. If we survive, we can do it all proper and by the book." He pockets the 'scope and, leaning heavily on the staff that provides both support and light, picks up a tool, ready to face the monumental mechanical triage before him.

Our friend is certainly experienced, having been through many battles. He knows how to spot an oncoming attack, how to fight well, and how to survive in dire circumstances. He is something of a magician, repairing machines with spit and determination. He will always be ready to take the last stand...and likely survive to take the next last stand.

Sometimes, if the situation warrants, it is wise to be ready for an attack, or to be willing and able to fight to

the last breath. We saw this in the Seven of Wands. Does this beguiling, rough warrior, though, live too much in suspicion and paranoia, seeing attackers and danger where there are none? Has his passion for survival squelched his will to live?

If the Nine of Wands appears in your reading, you are preparing to take a "last stand" in your life—and you will survive. After this crisis, take some time to reflect on your mindset. Has your passion for drama and love of overcoming insurmountable odds taken over your life? Are you surviving at the expense of living your life? The wands represent our will, and magically speaking, our will creates our reality (see the Three of Wands for a refresher on this). If your will is focused on constant attacks and an unending parade of foes, perhaps you are drawing them to you. It doesn't hurt to ask, does it?

TEN OF WANDS

· · · ·

"What is more burdensome: the past that is known or the future that is unknown?"

Core meaning: Carrying a large burden or many burdens.

Wands, the suit representing our will (and consequently our intent, choices, and actions), culminate in this poignant scene of experience gained and determination discovered.

She walks down the street, carrying her bundle of wands, each one representing the repercussions of choices she made or actions she took. The cards littering the path behind her are face-up, representing her conscious knowledge of her own past and how it has created her present situation. Both realizations weigh heavy on her, but, being a creature of wands, she does not despair. On the contrary, she discovers her own inner determination, strength, and power. Shouldering what she created, her responsibilities, she uses her experience to light her way forward, bravely stepping onto the next as-yet-unrevealed card and into the unknown.

When this card turns up, it quite simply describes a burdensome time. But do not be distracted, for there is nothing simple about it, and there is much for you to learn now. Although this is not the most pleasant of experiences, you should not be surprised by anything, as it is of your own design. An honest look at your own actions will show you exactly how you came to this place. The Ten of Wands invites you to use that knowledge to light your way as you move ahead in your life, and to tap into the strength you've developed along the way. You may not be thrilled with the present, but you can make good use of it to ensure that your future is more to your liking.

ACE OF CUPS

••••

"It contains, it dispenses. It cleanses,
it heals. It really is dead useful.
The only thing is, I'm not exactly
clear on how to work it."

Core meaning: An opportunity for an
emotional experience or growth.

In tarot, the element of water, which is associated with the suit of cups, is a powerful symbol. Take a quick trip through the cups cards and you will see that they deal with emotions and relationships. The dramatic stories of love and loss, joy and despair, romance and friendship are told in these images. The cups cards represent our feelings and relationships, which are the ways we experience water, that element that flows into, through, and around our life.

Water is a particularly rich symbol. On one hand, it represents our subconscious and our dreaming self, existing below consciousness. This connection is especially clear when we think of the ocean and the strange, colorful, and alien world that exists beneath its surface. In literature, water often represents the soul. And, for those who believe in a higher being, it is the cleansing grace of the Divine. Water is linked, whether scientifically true or not, to the moon via the ocean tides, a relationship that heightens the mysterious, untamed aspect of this element.

All that water represents is by nature hard to understand or to describe. We feel things deeply, but we don't always

know why. As Blaise Pascal said, "The heart has reasons that reason can never understand."

The suit of cups explores this vague yet powerful world—both the cups themselves, which are our ways of ordering and understanding our experiences of water, and the element of water and all that it represents. We begin with the ace, the pure form and expression of the suit.

The cup itself is finely crafted, expressing both beauty and practicality. Representing our ideal relationship with the element of water, it is perfectly balanced in its intake of water and its outpouring. There is neither too much nor too little. The gold dove on top, blessing the cup and its contents, communicates the intent: the pure receiving and expression of the truest feelings of the heart through a relationship with the Divine. The gears and clockwork on the cup are a nod to the human brain's need for patterns and order. This is a perfectly balanced system and as such takes into account human requirements. The water constantly flows in, keeping the cup filled with fresh water. The water flows out and nourishes the surrounding lotus flowers, meaning that the outpouring of our hearts feeds the spiritual enlightenment of those around us.

As you may imagine, humans are not often in this perfect state of grace and balance. When this card blesses your reading, look for a tender gift from the universe. This will likely be an opportunity to experience, either through giving or receiving or even both, an unexpected gift of love or other deep emotional connection. Aces always represent fleeting moments. When it makes an appearance, act on it, for it will quickly fade away.

TWO OF CUPS

. . . .

**"You say chemistry; I say magic.
Let's not allow semantics to
destroy this moment."**

Core meaning: Deep emotional
connection or attraction.

Some say that emotions are nothing more than chemical reactions based on our ancient "fight, flight, freeze, or faint" instincts. Some say that our emotions are rooted in our connection with the Divine. Others suggest that our emotions are the chemical reactions, while our feelings are how we package those emotions to fit into our culture and personal worldview. All of this may be very interesting—or perhaps mind-numbingly dull. And it is mostly all moot.

Because, really, who can deny that when the right eyes meet and hands touch, there is a sizzle that is palpable to anyone paying attention, particularly those directly involved. Is it chemistry? Magic? Fate? Destiny? Or, as Annie's brother in *Sleepless in Seattle* said, "Annie, when you're attracted to someone, it just means that your subconscious is attracted to their subconscious, subconsciously. So what we think of as fate is just two neuroses knowing that they are a perfect match."

Whatever you call it, that's what this card heralds: two people crossing paths and knowing that there is something more to it than meets the eye. Here a young man and a young woman openly offer their cups and all they contain to each other. Symbolically, cups are related to cauldrons. Cauldrons are more than just containers; they are places where magical transformations occur. When our two young people pour the waters of their hearts and souls together, a chemical reaction—or magic—takes place, and something entirely new is created. Being magical Victorians, they'd probably call it alchemy.

While a romantic partnership is certainly possible when this card appears in a reading, it is not the only option. Any potential partnership can be represented here. The most important element is that when the two people come together, they create something unique and powerful.

• • • •

Reading tip: If the question is specifically about finding new love, the Two of Cups is a clear indication that romance is definitely, ahem, in the cards.

THREE OF CUPS

• • • •

"So these three women walk
into a bar: a researcher, an
aviatrix, and a fortuneteller..."

Core meaning: A spontaneous,
unexpected joy or pleasure.

Throughout human history, trinities have played important
roles spiritually, magically, and in storytelling, including
TV shows and jokes. Writing and slogans are more powerful when they incorporate what is called the Rule of Three.
According to this precept, in the first instance a tension is
created, it is built up in the second, and then released in the
third. This is strangely satisfying to the human soul, apparently. The Three of Cups is a marvelous expression of the
Rule of Three.

The sets of threes in this image create a richly layered
moment of satisfaction. On the surface, it looks like a
happy, spontaneous moment—three women enjoying the
present. However, this present moment is not completely
spontaneous, nor does it exist in isolation. The pictures on
the wall indicate their past achievements. The items on the
table show their intentions for the future. The present contains the past as well as the future, a happy triad of time.
The three types of women bring three different energies to
the moment. Their differences are expressed not only in
their clothing but also in the cups, or vessels, they hold.

While they are all sharing an emotional moment, their experiences are different. The differences, however, do not cause conflict. On the contrary, the differences make the whole experience richer.

If this card shows up somewhere in your past, present, or future, you have enjoyed or will enjoy one of these excellent moments. You will be with people you care about, celebrating and honoring not your accomplishments but each other. This is a card of recognizing and luxuriating in the ties that bind and drinking deeply of the wine of friendship. Your collective past has brought you to this moment. While this card does show a literal moment, keep in mind that the tarot is symbolic and metaphoric. Consequently, in your reading, this card can refer to a group of supportive friends on whom you should rely. Fortified by the strength you find in each other, you look forward to the future with confidence.

• • • •

Reading tip: The Three of Cups can represent a party of women, such as a girls' night or a bridal or baby shower.

FOUR OF CUPS

• • • •

"No, I don't want any tea. Can't
you see that I am busy?"

Core meaning: Dissatisfaction with reality.

Some numbers have very strong associations. Four is such a number, and it resonates with stability, sturdiness, and reliability. The four-sided shape, the square, sometimes implies good, honest, and proper, as in "a square deal." However, during the Jazz Age, *square* came to mean "stuffy" or "old-fashioned" and was used to describe people who didn't keep up with the cultural times—in other words, those who were culturally stagnant. The negative extreme of stability is stagnation.

Let us look at the card and its depiction of this fine gentleman as he gazes upon his three very fine chalices. He's been looking at them for a very long time. If we watch long enough, perhaps we'll see a spider spin a web off the edge of his shoe. The longer he stares, the unhappier he becomes. He is the very picture of ennui, and what is ennui but emotions in stagnation?

Although his situation looks safe, this state can be deceptively dangerous. Nothing is being achieved. The disillusion and boredom sap all energy. If he continues in this manner, he will feel too weary to rouse himself. Mired down in the muck of dullness, our fine friend could lose any zest for life, becoming like the living dead. Perhaps that skull on the shelf is a well-placed warning. Likely he'll never see it, though, or that extraordinary chalice nearby.

If you find this card in your reading, you might want to be wiser than the man in the picture and take it as a warning. Boredom and dissatisfaction are normal experiences in life. Life is not always thrilling. How long, though, should you brood over such disappointments? At what point does feeling listless stop being an emotion and start being a choice? Ah, but this card is not a sermon. It simply lets you know that the ennui is present in the situation. What you choose to do with that information is entirely up to you. But there is that skull in the picture...

FIVE OF CUPS

• • • •

"I told him not to mind about the mess. But he was too far into his sobbing and couldn't leave off."

Core meaning: Experience of loss and grief.

Regret for mistakes made that cannot be unmade. Missing a past that can never be recovered. Crying over spilt milk. In the suit of cups, the cups are how we hold, contain, and organize our emotions. The liquid they contain is raw emotion. When a cup has been toppled—knocked over by our own carelessness or dashed from our hand by someone else—the emotions, the liquid, pour out, dripping to the ground and seeping back into the earth. Try as we might, we'll never get that liquid, in the same whole and pure form, back into the cup, no matter how valiant our attempts. Whatever we had before is completely and utterly gone.

Remember the Ace of Cups and the constant flow in and out of the cup? That is our ideal state of being. Whenever we find our cups empty, they will, in time, be filled again.

In this image, a compassionate barmaid watches with sympathy as her customer is racked with loss. His pain is almost as hard for her to witness as it is for him to experience. She, standing to his right, represents the future and all that it has to offer. But he is not ready for a new glass of anything. His head, his mind, his focus is all to the left,

the past. Remembering the sweetness of the past makes the present, the spilled cups, all the more bitter.

When you get this card, approach the situation with tenderness. This is a time of deep sadness and loss. Feelings are raw and intense. We do like to gloss over these situations, diverting our attention to promises of a better future and happy moments ahead. That will come, in time. For now, take a cue from the barmaid: be on hand with libations and sympathy. There are times when there is nothing to be done except have a good long cry.

• • • •

Reading tip: While mourning a loss is normal, if there is concern about extreme or unhealthy lengths of depression, watch for the Ten of Swords or the Moon along with this card.

SIX OF CUPS

· · · ·

"In the midst of grime and despair, the smallest act becomes unspeakably beautiful."

Core meaning: Happy memories.

A dark corner in a reechy industrial neighborhood has a hidden oasis—a temporary flower shop. Behind ragged clothes are other unseen treasures: dreams that haven't fallen prey to reality, ideals about chivalry, hopes for the future, and shy vulnerability. In an unplanned moment, a memory is created. He will forever remember the sweet girl, beautiful despite her dirty face. She will look for generous kindness in the eyes of every man she meets. They will both know, always, that magic exists.

The cup he gives her contains flowers, symbolic of something lovely, delicate, and transitory. They will, in time, fade and die. But they will live on in memory, a reminder of the finer feelings that can spring up anywhere. Memories, though, are funny things and take on lives of their own. They are not entirely trustworthy, and people have been known to romanticize the past.

When this card shows up in your reading, a whisper from the past is influencing the situation. A kind act. A gentle touch. A quiet word. Memories, being the illusionary things that they are, can shape your experience in various ways.

This young couple could remind you that you are idealizing a past action, or they could be reminding you to move forward with spontaneous innocence, acting from the heart, with no analysis or concerns about future ramifications.

While this is an undeniably sweet card, it shares similarities with the Moon card. Our lovely dream worlds of nostalgia are often infused with confusion, light as mist and easily ignored.

SEVEN OF CUPS

· · · ·

"In this moment all possible futures
exist—until you pick one."

Core meaning: Dreams and desires.

In Margaret Atwood's postapocalyptic novel *The Handmaid's Tale*, women are told that the new government makes their lives better because it gives them "freedom from choice." Freedom from making choices does have a certain appeal. Making decisions can be exhausting. Who hasn't, at some point, said, "Oh, I really don't care…can you just decide?" Picking something that you want should be an easy task. If pressed, most people would prefer that to the alternative, of having all their choices made by someone else. Unfortunately, picking one thing over another is not always that easy. The sense of responsibility and fear of making a wrong move looms over us.

The Seven of Cups captures a person in the midst of a moment of choice. Cups of potential possibilities parade before his eyes, slowly enough so that he can consider each one. All have something of value; all stir his imagination and speak to his heart…this is, after all, the suit of cups; his emotions are utterly engaged. He could easily spend the afternoon here, lost in daydreams. Decisions are arrived at in different ways. Careful thought, a detailed analysis of the pros and cons, and projecting into the future are all part of

the process. We learned in the Justice card that our current choices create our future, so we want to select wisely.

And yet there are times when logic doesn't play as large a role as we like to think. When our creativity and emotions are involved, the situation can get a bit fuzzy. Fears based in past experiences cause negative reactions to perfectly suitable choices. Dreams, desires, and romantic notions cast an attractive haze over certain options.

This beguiling card reflects all the complexities of having an abundance of possibilities. Will our young man become so caught up in his speculations and fantasies that he neglects to act at all? If he delays long enough, maybe some possibilities will disappear. Of course, perhaps others will appear.

When this card shows up in your readings, think about how long you are willing to stand motionless and transfixed by the wondrous potential of your life before lifting a cup and taking that first sip of a fresh adventure.

• • • •

Reading tip: This card can represent confusion or living in a fantasy world, particularly if the Moon or Two of Swords is present.

$$\left[\frac{-\hbar^2}{2m}\nabla^2 + V\right]\Psi = i\hbar\frac{\partial}{\partial t}\Psi$$

$$\sqrt{\infty}$$

EIGHT OF CUPS

• • • •

"Knowing where you are is important. Knowing where you are supposed to be is imperative."

Core meaning: Leaving something behind to search for something else.

She found the mechanism, studied its intricacies. Cleaned, polished, repaired. She determined exactly what it was created to do. She understood precisely what it measured, as well as how to accurately analyze the information. The strange relationship between her, the extraordinary astrolabe, and the wisdom it revealed was, in theory, quite perfect—a dream come true. But in reality, it was not.

She knew what this life was supposed to feel like, and she knew what it did feel like. The ideal and the reality were not the same. With a certainty born of perfect understanding and undeniable experience, she did what she had to. Leaving was hard, but she told herself that her investment of time, love, and skill was not wasted. Without it, she never would have known where she needed to be.

Life is funny. You can be living the dream and yet be unhappy. Part of the journey is realizing that dreams are not "one size fits all." No matter how many people agree on any single perfect life, there really isn't one that is meant for everyone. If you are looking at this card in your reading, you know all too well what it means. You've been living a dream. But it isn't yours, at least not anymore. But you could only know this by experiencing it for yourself. Nothing is lost; no investment is wasted. You will bring all that you gained with you as you move toward your new destination—with sadness, perhaps, but also with certainty.

• • • •

Reading tip: The message to leave a situation is emphasized if the Six of Swords, the Fool, the Chariot, or any of the knights are present.

NINE OF CUPS

· · · ·

**"Come in and welcome! Your
every desire will be served with a
warm smile. Order carefully."**

Core meaning: Material, emotional,
and physical well-being.

Back in the old days of fortunetelling with tarot, tarot readers told you to make a silent wish before beginning your reading. If the Nine of Cups showed up in your reading, it meant that the wish you made at the beginning would come true. Looking at this warm and welcoming image, full of promise and fun, it is easy to see how this came to be known as the wish card.

Our lovely hostess evokes the feeling that anything you want is available to you and that she is here to grant your wishes. Because the focus is on the happy hostess, one cannot help but wonder who gains the most. She is in the position of granting her customer's desires. Does she get as much or even more pleasure in granting wishes as the guests do in receiving them? When we see this card, we are reminded that wishes are just as complex as people and can be granted in many (and sometimes unexpected) ways.

All in all, if this card is present in a reading, it brings very happy and bountiful energy with it—although isn't there an old saying about wishes? "If wishes were horses,

then beggars would ride"—no, not that one. Oh, yes: "Be careful what you wish for."

• • • •

Reading tip: If the card appears with the Sun, the Wheel of Fortune, or the Ace of Pentacles, I'd go buy a lottery ticket. If it is accompanied by the Devil, be wary of dangerous overindulgence.

TEN OF CUPS

• • • •

"This is it: right here, right now.
This is the heart of my life."

Core meaning: Happy home.

Ensconced in their garden, this couple enjoys a quiet moment stolen from the midst of one of the busy days that typifies their life. Their little bower area creates their respite from the world. Symbolically, this is their shared center: the heart of their relationship, their home, and their lives. It is their Ace of Cups, a place of ever-flowing love and healing.

One may wonder how they were so lucky to find such easy happiness. While they are indeed fortunate, they did not simply stumble into this life. Again, recall that in the suit of cups, the cups represent our ways of ordering and understanding our experiences of water. A couple begins with the Ace of Cups, the first flowing of attraction, and the Two of Cups, two hearts recognizing each other. Over time, that emotion must wend itself through all the complexities of both partners and every aspect of their lives. Crafting a system that allows for the free flow of love does not happen by accident. The intricate arch above our lovers shows their creation. Through the years, they've worked together to devise a reality that is beautiful and that works for both of them.

If this card graces your reading, consider the implications of long-term relationships that successfully weave together many strands and create an exquisite tapestry. Is such a relationship your reality? Your hope? Your goal? If you have it, bravo! Well done. If you want it, be prepared to roll up your proverbial sleeves and start building. Like Rome, domestic bliss cannot be built in a day.

• • • •

Reading tip: This card is often associated with marriage, particularly if the Lovers, the Hierophant, the Four of Wands, or the Two of Cups is present.

ACE OF SWORDS

• • • •

"As the great bard said, there is nothing either good nor bad, but thinking makes it so."

Core meaning: An opportunity for a new way of thinking.

The suit of swords is always dramatic. Flip through these cards and you will see images depicting problems (and sometimes their solutions), philosophies, ethical dilemmas, and the power of the stories we tell ourselves. Symbolically, these cards deal with two human functions: thinking and communicating. The way we think about a situation often determines whether or not we consider it a problem. By establishing an expectation of the way things are supposed to be, we usually create our own problems. Once we create or identify our challenges, we then use reason to solve or to decide how to react to them.

In tarot, swords are associated with the element of air. Air, as a symbol, is connected with the word *logos,* which means (among other things) words, reasons, order, and knowledge. It is not a long leap from the Greek *logos* to our word *logic.* Many cultures in the world today value this way of understanding the world. It is associated with science and therefore with truth. If there really was just one "truth," wouldn't we all arrive at that same conclusion? Unfortunately, we do not all follow the same pristine and

infallible logic to the same inexorable conclusions. Instead we tell ourselves stories about our reality, which then create or sustain what we call "truth."

The sword in tarot is the sword of truth, the sword of reason, and the sword of knowledge. It cuts through the Gordian knots of our lives, allowing us to make decisions with confidence. Simply by saying the right things, we can console or heal another. Logic, reason, and words can become weapons in our hands when used to defend our position, tear down another's ideas, or carelessly or perhaps cruelly wound someone. The swords in tarot are clearly of the double-edged variety.

The Ace of Swords here is a finely wrought piece. That is something to keep in mind with all the swords…they are made. Language, truth, and even logic are human creations. Everything that we are and ever have been as individuals, cultures, and humans comes together to create a noosphere and how we think about the world and our place in it. In this image, complex devices and machines work together to create a deceptively simple yet beautiful sword.

If you receive the Ace of Swords, you have a wonderful opportunity to realize a truth that has been eluding you, to discover a solution to a problem, or to gain much-needed understanding about something. The truth, it is said, will set you free. This is a gift. Like all the best swords, this one is indeed double-edged. While it is a thing of beauty, it is also powerful, and you must learn to handle it carefully. Like all aces, it represents an opportunity that can disappear as quickly as a thought.

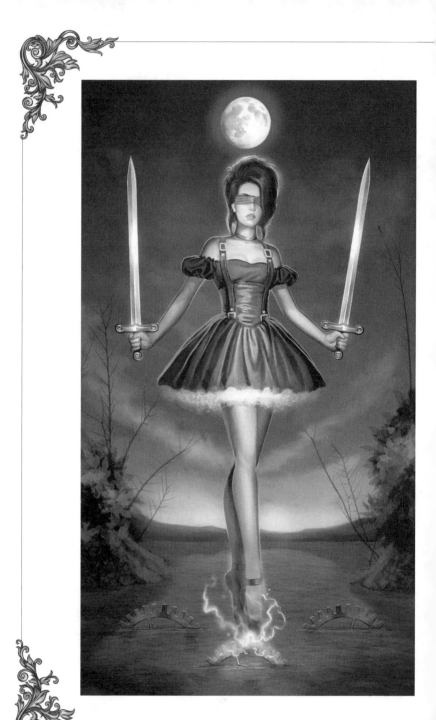

TWO OF SWORDS

• • • •

*"La-la-la-la-la-la-la—I can't hear
you. Just a bit occupied at the
moment. Please go away."*

Core meaning: A conflict
between heart and mind.

An unsettling blend of gracefulness and tension, she balances delicately between the water and the moon, keeping her swords aloft. Although artful, this activity takes up all her time and energy. The swords, representing her reason and her logic as well as the stories she tells herself about her life, require constant attention. Her environment is comprised largely of water, symbolic of her subconscious, and the moon, also connected with the darker aspects of the self. No wonder she prefers a blindfold. She is not caught between a rock and a hard place. Quite the opposite…she is dangling between water and air. Eventually she will tire, and something will give way. She will have to take off the blindfold, take stock of her situation, and make a decision. For now, though, she is doing remarkably well in ignoring her situation.

If you are feeling between and betwixt, the Two of Swords will probably show up in your reading. It lets you know that while you may feel like you are doing everything you can, you actually are spending too much energy accomplishing nothing. You are keeping busy and distracted while time passes, hoping that the situation will resolve itself. Cease for a moment. Breathe. Let your thoughts stop flailing. Take a look at where you are. Yes, you may have to face some fears or admit some unpleasant circumstances. You'll have to decide where you want to go and then figure out how to get there—it'll probably be less exhausting and more productive. Or keep holding your pose. Whatever works for you.

THREE OF SWORDS

• • • •

*"The misuse of tools can
lead to a mickle mess."*

Core meaning: Sorrow caused by knowledge.

Words can build bridges, create connections, and nurture relationships. Through careful communication, we can establish elaborate edifices of understanding that are stunningly beautiful and utterly awesome. All of these activities take time and skill.

In the smallest of moments, a few words can destroy what took years to create. Whether the words are cruel or merely careless, whether a painful truth or a manipulative deceit, the injury is very real.

In the shadows of a dark and stormy night, what was once a perfectly balanced, functional, and lovely clockwork heart lies in shambles. Straight, unyielding swords have been jammed ruthlessly through the delicate curves of fine craftsmanship, creating a poignant picture of tragic destruction.

The suit of swords is nothing if not dramatic, and the Three of Swords is no exception. The lofty and theatrical tendencies of our minds are here joined with the melodramatic and unpredictable characteristics of our hearts. Because the swords are wielded by another person's hand, the sense of betrayal and shock creates a raw, gaping wound.

Experiencing the Three of Swords is never fun. When your heart is stabbed, no doubt there will be pain. The wounds will heal, but even still, things will never be the same. However, lessons will be learned. Truths will be revealed. Understanding will occur. This card marks a sad time, but as with all experiences, you have the ability to determine how you will think about it, experience it, and ultimately fold it into your worldview.

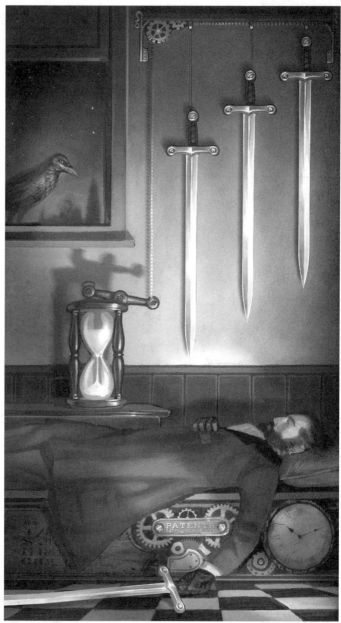

FOUR OF SWORDS

• • • •

"Don't be misled. That is a lot harder than it looks."

Core meaning: Respite from troubles.

We may question the wisdom of enjoying a nap while in the midst of a tricky or dangerous situation. This man, however, appears to be doing just that. A closer look at the situation may convince us that this course of action is actually an excellent choice.

The circumstances or events that are set in motion, represented by the three swords hanging from the ceiling, are going to happen. The hourglass lets us know that it is just a matter of time. Because we see three swords aimed at his head and body, we assume he logically concluded that no good will come of these events. While he has imagined how the situation will play out, he has clearly not thought of a way to stop or change the course of events.

In similar situations, do you flail about, frustrated and anxious, because you have to do something, anything? Our ability to project into and imagine the future is a function of our minds. This ability is a double-edged sword. While imagining the future, we are prone to either hope or worry. When our minds are tangled up with thoughts and fear, it is hard to hear inspired solutions whispered to our souls.

By taking a time-out and quieting our minds, we are more likely to receive a divine message or inspired solution.

Swords correspond to the element of air, as do birds of all sorts, such as the raven on the windowsill. Birds often symbolize messages from the heavens or other divine sources. Ravens don't generally enter a space if swords are flying around. When this card shows up in a reading, remember: still the swords, still the mind. The problems will continue to exist, but you'll be able to see them with different eyes.

FIVE OF SWORDS

· · · ·

**"He may have all the swords now,
but I warrant someone will find
something else to stab in his back."**

Core meaning: A victory tinged with defeat.

Who doesn't love success? After all, it is a "winner take all"
world, isn't it? And we all know that to the victor go the
spoils. This is probably why we enjoy playing games. The
rules and the terms of winning are clearly defined; everyone
involved knows all the consequences of any possible action.
If only reality were so simple. The game of life is much longer, much broader, and much, much more complicated than
any other game could ever be.

Take our contestants here in the Five of Swords. The man
in the fine red coat with the impressive sword-collecting
device and even more impressive top hat looks like the winner in this game. He seems to think that the goal is to take
the swords away from everyone. If that's true, he is indeed
doing a fine job. The other players don't look at all pleased;
most losers don't.

When a game is over, all the pieces are put away and
the players move on to other pastimes—unless they are bad
sports, in which case they'll likely sulk a bit. Real life is
never over in the way a game is over. In life, when people
feel like they've "lost" in some way, they often try to figure

out ways to regain what they gave up or what was taken from them.

If you find the Five of Swords in your reading, take a careful look at the situation. Watch for manipulation, trickery, and bullying. It is possible that someone is not playing fair. Perhaps you are the one who seems to be winning. This card advises you to look beyond the immediate success. Consider repercussions in the future. Your victory may cost more than it is worth.

SIX OF SWORDS

• • • •

"A lady always knows when it's time to leave."

Core meaning: Leaving a situation with help.

So many of the aspects of the suit of swords and the element of air come into play in this card: problems, decisions, quick action. The woman in the airship is escaping a bad (or unhealthy) situation. Having decided that this is the best way to deal with her problem (or challenge), she is moving quickly. We can almost feel the rush of cold air and the precariousness of the fabric, ropes, and basket that comprise the ship. Imagine the wind blowing the fear and anxiety off her. Imagine her future becoming clearer with each moment.

Being in a bad situation is hard enough. Deciding the best way to resolve it and finding the courage to do so is even harder, especially when in the midst of a crisis. In addition, there are times when resolving the situation or making an escape cannot be done alone, and help is needed. Asking for help when feeling desperate is hard for some people, making a stressful situation even more so.

When this vehicle arrives to pick you up, don't hesitate to jump in. The situation you find yourself in is not going to change, so it's time for you to move on. You'll need help. Ask for it. Be brave. Be decisive. Feel the winds of change, and gaze into a fresh future.

• • • •

Reading tip: If the Chariot or any of the knights are present, the suggestion for quick action is emphasized.

SEVEN OF SWORDS

· · · ·

"Who is the thief, and what
exactly is being stolen?"

Core meaning: Someone has taken something.

Stepping lightly through the mist, a young thief steals away
with a bundle of swords. Her colorful clothing contradicts
her stealthy movements. She is not properly garbed for
melting silently into the shadows. One wonders what she
was thinking.

Glancing backwards, she has the impression that the
eye crowning the door behind her is watching her, marking her actions. The building represents society. She is outside of society, at least right now, yet it sees her and judges
her. Perhaps that is why she is dressed so strangely. She is
asserting her uniqueness, her separateness from the group.
Even if the swords are hers, even if she is simply refusing
to participate in society, society does consider that a theft, a
weakening of the whole.

Being an individual, being true to yourself, is important. It is part of our spiritual journey. However, if the thief
shows up in your reading, consider your motivations. What
are you taking away with you and why? Is it for the greatest
good? Who are you hurting in the process? Is this really a
step forward in your journey? Unfortunately, in basic terms,
this card can also represent someone else taking something
that belongs to you.

EIGHT OF SWORDS

· · · ·

**"It is easier to solve a problem
if you can see it clearly."**

Core meaning: A precarious situation.

Her bound hands may be immobile, but they can still feel the luxurious, finely woven silk of her skirt. She hears slight whispers, the soft touch of metal on metal when precisely tooled components lock together and move apart. The scent of her own fear coats her nostrils. The back of her tongue shivers with the metallic taste of anxiety. The short, sharp gusts of the moving blades generate soft wisps of air that touch her face, shoulders, and hands, and flutter her skirt at random intervals. She tells herself that they cannot really touch her, but each gust cuts her like a sword. Every sense is heightened save the one she is denied: sight.

Unable to see her surroundings, every sensation is sharply unexpected. Looking at her, paralyzed by and glistening with her own fear, it is an easy thing to judge her. For there is surely a way of escape, if only she would focus. That is the point, though: she cannot see, literally and metaphorically. Trapped by her own thoughts, her way of looking at the situation has created a prison from which there is no escape.

The Eight of Swords represents a doubly precarious situation. If this card shows up in your reading, it is likely that the reality is problematic, and resolving it satisfactorily would be a challenge in any case. The trouble is probably exacerbated by your way of looking at it, or perhaps it is more accurate to say that you are not looking at it. You are sensing in other ways, but you are not seeing things clearly.

NINE OF SWORDS

· · · ·

"The long, dark teatime of the soul isn't nearly as romantic as one imagines."

Core meaning: The power of worry and regret.

Who hasn't experienced the unkindness, even the downright cruelty, of others? While that experience is bad enough, no one can torture you with quite the same precision as you can torture yourself. Hidden below the surface, in your subconscious, all your worries, despair, and guilt churn during the day. Then, in the quiet stillness of the night, they shake you awake. Emerging from the dark ocean of your fears, they take wing and become conscious thoughts.

These strange birds, these bizarre and frightening creations of your mind, flit about, pecking and poking at you. Each entry wound gets deeper, and the birds either grow huge or multiply. And there you are, alone in the dark with a flock of custom-designed monsters.

At its best, the suit of swords represents logic, rational thought, understanding, and truth. Thoughts, though, are not always rational. Truth is not absolute but rather can be created. We know that if someone hears something often enough, they come to accept it as true. On a Nine of Swords night, we can literally convince ourselves of anything. Why is it always something horrible?

If the Nine of Swords threatens your sleep, remember that this experience is entirely your own doing. The good

news is that you can stop it. This knowledge is also somewhat maddening, because there is no easy answer for ending this vicious cycle. Often a flurry of irrational thoughts can be subdued by applying logic. Separate the birds, looking at just one at a time. If something can be done about any particular bird, resolve to do it at the first possible opportunity. If there is nothing that can be done, practice releasing such thoughts. Or you can continue building your flock...

TEN OF SWORDS

· · · ·

"Well, thank goodness that's over."

Core meaning: Surrender to unpleasant
or unfortunate circumstances.

As mentioned earlier, the suit of swords is always dramatic, and its grand finale in the ten is no exception. The sun begins to rise (or is it setting?), covering the scene with a bloody shadow. How is it that one finds oneself lying on a roof, every limb skewered? This is quite disheartening, especially after the long climb to the top of the building. Despite the tragic finality of this situation, we can find some wisdom and advice here. Probably no one is going to be literally stabbed.

The truth that promised to set you free in the Ace of Swords has gone horribly wrong. Your thoughts, ideas, or realizations—your weapons to cut through the chaos and confusion of life—have turned on you. The complex worldview you created and that helped you function in life has collapsed upon itself, or you turned it on yourself. Instead of using thoughts and logic to move forward, you're using them as an excuse for immobility, for playing the victim, for seeing problems at every turn. Maybe someone decided to turn their truths against you, which might manifest as hate, prejudice, or cruelty.

What makes this experience look awful also contains beauty. The image looks frightening because it looks like "the end." The sun is playing two symbolic roles (a common practice of symbols, by the way). We see the setting sun and know that the end of this experience is at hand. We see the rising sun and know that a new day is dawning—that within this (and every) ending is a new beginning.

Look next to his left hand. The final card has been played. It really is over.

ACE OF PENTACLES

• • • •

"How does it feel to hold the potential of the world in your hand?"

Core meaning: An opportunity for prosperity.

The pentacles represent our physical life. As such, they may seem, to the uninitiated, to be the most mundane of the suits. But consider that the pentacle represents the physical manifestation of spirit. Similarly, the figure of Jesus is also said to be the Christian god made flesh. Come to think of it, there were those who thought him to be a bit too earthy and mundane to be holy, what with all those tarts and all that wine.

Earth is the element associated with this suit, and its most obvious qualities are stability, form, and security. The element of earth shares some characteristics with the number four and with the Emperor, cards that help shape our lives. In addition, earth brings us abundance and so reflects the world of the Empress. The element of earth supplies the resources that meet our physical needs. It is also connected with our worldly status, our mastery over the physical world, and the way we interact with and the value we assign to these items.

The suit of pentacles explores the physical world and how we shape it, how it shapes us, and how we interact with it and with each other in it. This is the suit where everyday life is lived. As Benjamin Franklin said: "Do not

squander time. That is the stuff that life is made of." Time is also an important resource and is also represented by these cards.

The Ace of Pentacles shows a complex mechanized hand bestowing the gift of a shiny pentacle. Arthur Edward Waite, the designer of the famous and groundbreaking Rider-Waite-Smith Tarot (published in 1909), said that this card was the most favorable card in the deck. He doesn't say why, but I believe it is because it represents a gift of pure and amazing luck, an opportunity that can explode into undreamed-of abundance and accomplishment. If you peek ahead to the Nine and Ten of Pentacles, you'll see what I mean. There are those who say we make our own luck. The mechanized hand represents our role in creating our own lucky opportunities and in nurturing those possibilities to fruition.

Safely ensconced in a lovely garden, the Ace of Pentacles is a seed. As it shines, we think of not just its material potential but also its divine spark.

When you get this card, consider it your lucky day. Look sharp for the opportunity that is right in front of you, and make the most of it. If you cannot see any such opportunity in your life, think about what can be done to create your own luck.

• • • •

Reading tip: All of the aces are good omens and bring favorable energy to a situation, but the Ace of Pentacles holds even more promise. It uplifts all the cards in a spread.

TWO OF PENTACLES

• • • •

"I think I can, I think I can, I think I can..."

Core meaning: Maintaining balance.

Merely riding one of those pennyfarthing bicycles would be hard enough, but to ride it across water seems impossible. How and why is she compelled to do this? The answer isn't simple, but the lemniscate holds a key to this mystery. We've seen this before—in the Magician, the High Priestess, and the Strength cards. This interesting symbol represents the infinite flow of the universe. In tarot, it usually speaks to the union of (or the relationship between) opposites. In the Magician, there is the relationship between above and below (in terms of "As above, so below"). In Strength, it is the delicate dance between the self and the shadow.

In the Two of Pentacles, we see the relationship between available resources (such as time and energy) and perceived need. She exerts great will and strength (reminiscent of the Magician and Strength) in order to retain this balance. If this card rides into your reading, you'll find yourself hard-pressed to balance everything that you feel needs balancing. Oh, you can and will do it. Maybe not for long, but for as long as necessary.

Determining what must be balanced brings up another important question. The water over which she rides so furiously should be considered. Water represents emotions, and it is the presence of this water that creates the need pictured here. She feels that she needs to do this. It is a perceived need, not necessarily a real need. Do a quick reality check in your life. Do you really need to do everything you think or feel you need to?

THREE OF PENTACLES

· · · ·

"What does it take to create a thing of substance and beauty?"

Core meaning: A goal is manifesting.

He consults his schematics for details about setting the final pentacle. The oracle searches the cards for nuances of wisdom. The craftswoman heeds their advice until she feels the materials respond to her touch. This is the team tasked with creating this cathedral, the union of spirit with the physical, the glory of the Divine cast in stone and glass.

The engineer, with his detailed and precise designs, represents the logic and science required to ensure that such a grand undertaking holds together and does not collapse under the weight of its own dreams. The oracle connects with the soul of the Divine and brings the inspiration, the vision, and the passion that gives the creation life. The craftswoman, using strong but sensitive hands, finds and releases the Divine living within the materials, bringing the structure from the realm of imagination to the plane of reality. Together they create extraordinary magic.

While this card can and often does indicate working together as a team to produce something, it can also be metaphoric. We all have within us the ability to be inspired, to acquire knowledge, and to gain skills and experience. When we combine all three of these, we usually create our

best work. This can, therefore, be a reminder to rely on a balanced approach to projects.

If this card appears in your reading, whatever you are working on has the potential to be something more than adequate. All the elements are there—whether within yourself or in the team that you are working with—to make something that will make you proud.

• • • •

Reading tip: If the Magician appears with this card, it suggests a solitary undertaking.

FOUR OF PENTACLES

• • • •

"Is a penny saved always a
penny earned, or is it sometimes
a penny wasted?"

Core meaning: Gathering power.

Her hand is white, smooth, and soft. Adorned with jewels
and fine silk lace, it enjoys all the finer things in life, even
though it has never, excuse the pun, lifted a finger to do the
hard work. If asked, she will share her secret to success.
"Never spend a single penny that you don't have to. Put
away everything you can." To demonstrate, she asks you for
a coin, which you hand over, a bewildered expression on
your countenance. Her elegant fingers clasp your coin while
her other hand winds a key on the side of a curious box. A
mechanical hand emerges and reaches out. She places your
coin in its fingers. Quick as a wink, the lid snaps shut—and
your coin is gone. It has joined the pile of wealth you can
see through box's glass panel.

It was just a coin. And it is a good lesson: saving is a
wise thing. And yet something about the experience was
slightly sickening.

Remember fours are about stability. Being related to
earth, pentacles also are stable. Combine the two and the
stability takes on a grotesque feeling.

Tarot shares the wisdom of the universe, which we see
in symbols like the lemniscate or the yin/yang symbol and

which are about the constant flow of energy. Stagnation and inertia lead to rot and death. Death is part of the life cycle and as such has value. That is the key: it is part of the life cycle. Cycles mean flow. When energy is prevented from flowing for too long, it feels unnatural. That's why the experience with the rich woman and the weird box gave you the heebie-jeebies.

If you get the Four of Pentacles in your reading, take a look at your relationship to your resources. It may be that you are in a situation requiring a little tightening of the belt. More likely, though, is the case that you are holding on too tightly. In your effort to make yourself safe and secure, you are actually cutting off the flow of energy, resources, and people into your life.

FIVE OF PENTACLES

· · · ·

"There is no sugarcoating it: these are hard times, very hard times indeed."

Core meaning: Physical need.

She feels the biting wind not as a discomfort to herself but as she imagines it feels to him. He is so much younger, so much weaker, than she. For his sake, she plunges into the wind and darkness and snow in search of safety and perhaps the slightest comfort.

What is more poignant than innocence facing the cruelty and neglect of the world? If anyone were to see such a plight, surely they would help, wouldn't they? This experience, while not as picturesquely displayed as this card, happens every day and often goes unalleviated. This is not a card of relief granted and mercies raining down from heaven. It is a card of need.

Steampunk worlds are created by the mash-up of genres. Here it looks like the stories of the little match girl (from Hans Christian Andersen's story of the same name) and Tiny Tim (a character from Dickens's *A Christmas Carol*) have collided in a tale of epic tragedy. The image of the suffering, abused, or neglected child is common in Victorian literature and art. The stories mentioned here were written only two years apart, in the mid-1800s. Some say that images of children became symbolic for the part of humanity that was sacrificed to feed the Industrial Revolution.

What of the church in the background; what symbolic role does it play? Is it help that is at hand but is overlooked or rejected by the children? Is it help from an institution that should be offered but is not, because the institution lost its vision and compassion? What is the relationship between the children's physical and spiritual lives?

When this card shows up in your reading, it describes a time of physical need. Money could be lacking, health could be in question, time might be nonexistent, or basic survival needs are perhaps not being met. This complex card does far more than describe the situation. It brings a pile of questions and unceremoniously drops them at your feet. As you work your way through them, you will likely find wise advice for improving your situation.

SIX OF PENTACLES

• • • •

"We cannot hurry this; we have our methods. The proper procedures must be followed."

Core meaning: Flowing material energy.

It is ironic that in this suit that deals with the element of earth—the most solid and stable of the elements—the idea of flow is so crucial. Perhaps it is because earth is so concrete that we need to be reminded that it, too, is really part of the energetic makeup of the universe. As we know from physics, even matter is mostly empty space.

As with most of the sixes, there is an emphasis on the flow of energy and on relationships. This image highlights the number six by showing two dynamic relationships consisting of three factors each. There are three people: one giving, one receiving, and one waiting to receive. There are three kinds of resources: the book from the recipient on one side of the scale, the equal exchange of coins on the other side, and the pile of coins that the lady controls. While quite a lot is going on in this deceptively sedate picture, the action and interaction of the relationships and the resources can be summed up in one word: reciprocity.

While you may think this is a card about simple charity, it is more complicated than that. The weighing of need, or of the application for resources, and the precise meting out of those resources suggests that the type of help given here is asked for. The people in need sought it out—made their need and desire for help known to those who can provide it. Those with the means then decide how and on whom to bestow their bounty.

The Six of Pentacles lets you know that help is at hand, but it won't just fall into your lap. Look around and see what avenues are available. Make your application to the best of your ability. Yes, someone's ego might not like this approach. Life lessons aren't always fun. On the other hand, if you are the one being approached to help meet a need, keep in mind how difficult it is to ask for help. Don't make it harder on the recipient than it already is.

SEVEN OF PENTACLES

....

"How does reality measure up to your expectations?"

Core meaning: Appraising results of efforts.

The room is silent save for the scratching of his pen as he makes notes and his occasional murmurings of "Hmmm... interesting" and "Fascinating" and "Mmmm...I didn't expect *that*."

He's kept careful notes from the beginning of this project: from the very first brainstorming of ideas, through myriad rejected plans, to the carefully delineated final grand scheme, noting each and every step along the way until now, the end of the adventure. Now is the time for the reckoning. Now is the time to answer many questions. Now is the time to make decisions based on those answers.

The Order of the Golden Dawn, a Victorian-era magical order, called this card "Success Unfulfilled." As you see, in the spirit of steampunkery, I've taken liberties with that notion. Everything rides on one's definition of "success," and I suspect that the fine gentlemen of the Golden Dawn were perfectionists. The problem with perfectionism is that it is attachment to a predetermined outcome. Victorians were also a mickle obsessed with progress, which perhaps they extrapolated to mean "motion." Because this card is a pause in progress, we can see why it would be unfulfilling to them.

We know, don't we, that stopping to assess our work is not a lack of progress but rather just another step toward success. And as the grand adventurers we are, we would never limit our ideas of success to a predetermined outcome. One never knows what unanticipated wonderfulness awaits.

If you draw this card, prepare yourself to draw up some notes. Whatever you are asking about, whatever you are working on right now, it is time to seriously assess the situation. Start by identifying what you had hoped to accomplish. Compare that to what has actually occurred to date. How does it measure up? Does it fall short? Does it exceed your wildest dreams? Now that you've put in the effort and you've experienced the results, was the investment worth it? What does all this mean for your next move? This card of quiet contemplation is going to require a lot of brainpower.

EIGHT OF PENTACLES

· · · ·

*"The quest for perfection can
be exhilarating. Exhausting,
but exhilarating!"*

Core meaning: Working carefully.

The steam generated by the huge machines surrounding her creates a dreamlike atmosphere, blurring the hard edges of the machines and softening the sound of the grinding gears. Although the din is muffled, the movement and noise is loudly distracting. In contrast, her world is utterly clear. She is completely oblivious to her environment—including, apparently, her coffee, which appears to have cooled and is in danger of falling off her workbench. Utterly engrossed with the task at hand, she examines her recent work, looking not only for flaws but also for unconscious improvements and the effects of new techniques. For although she is quite competent, she desires to become a master. She knows that it takes more than raw talent and more than dedication. It takes an eye for seeing how small changes can effect significant improvements in both process and the end result.

Most people work to earn their living. This is a card of that sort of work. But it is also more than that. The Eight of Pentacles is about loving the work itself and taking pride in doing it well. The desire to constantly improve is not so much to benefit the employer as it is to keep oneself engaged and satisfied. All of the eights explore the theme of movement. Here there is inner movement—the growth toward perfecting one's skills—in the midst of the external movement of our daily routines. Like our craftsperson, we learn to drown out what is not essential to our purposes.

When you get this card, remember that whatever improvements you make in your skill set are ultimately for your benefit. Whatever you achieve is for yourself. The Seven of Pentacles encourages you to challenge yourself and reach for a higher level of mastery.

NINE OF PENTACLES

• • • •

"Everyone wants to be me."

Core meaning: Accomplishment.

So many of my colleagues, as well as myself, identify with this card. For many entrepreneurial woman, this card represents the dream fulfilled—not the Ten of Cups or the Ten of Pentacles, the Nine of Pentacles. Why is that?

This card represents a self-made woman (or man). Through self-mastery, discipline, and hard work, she has created a safe, stable, secure, and rich life. Although not given to opulence and ostentation, she is committed to quality. Sometimes the well-crafted is more expensive than the well-decorated. She values discipline, symbolized here by the falcon. This bird sits on her arm as the result of dedicated training. Because of that training, it will not fly away. She is in control.

Independence is a very important element of this card. As a nine, it is associated with the Hermit, who has made his own way spiritually and is dependent on no one else. Our lady in the Nine of Pentacles has made not just a wonderful life but also one that she retains as much control over as is possible. Tower moments do happen, though, and so we know nothing is completely guaranteed.

It is this control and independence that makes this image such an alluring dream. The Ten of Cups and the Ten of Pentacles are contingent on other people. And no matter how

firm someone's commitment to a shared dream, you never really know when they will start desiring another path.

When your reading is graced with this card, make sure you appreciate it! The Nine of Pentacles is an excellent sign that life, right now, is quite good. You worked hard for everything you have. You have every right to indulge and enjoy it all.

• • • •

Reading tip: Self-sufficiency and independence are commendable goals. However, if this card comes up with the Hermit or the Chariot, perhaps you are taking things a little too far. Make sure you've not behaving in an extreme or unhealthy manner. Taking care of oneself does not mean being antisocial. One does have obligations to society.

TEN OF PENTACLES

· · · ·

"And they lived happily ever after."

Core meaning: Stable and abundant life.

Remember all the promises inherent in the Ace of Pentacles? Here they are, fully grown.

This image is a simple scene of domestic bliss and economic comfort. There is more represented here, though, a connection to spirit and to the cycles of life that adds richness and texture to their lives. The opulent home, under whose arch they are gathered, speaks of an old family home and consequently of roots and traditions that give our lives strong foundations and a sense of security that goes beyond a savings account. The dogs are loyalty and devotion. In the Nine of Pentacles we mentioned how it is not always easy to count on the dedication of another to one's dream. The dogs represent that, insofar as it is humanly possible, the people here are devoted to one another and the life they have created. The child, of course, hints at the future and of living with an eye to long-term happiness, not just indulging momentary desires.

The gypsy fortuneteller in the foreground flips the final card: the Ten of Diamonds, the poker deck's equivalent to the Ten of Pentacles. All the potential that was given to these people in the Ace of Pentacles has been fully realized. This moment is perfect and beautiful, and if this were a movie, we'd all be crying.

The shadowy secret of this card is that tens are endings. The promise of abundance has culminated here. Once it has been played, another card must be dealt, for life is a cycle, and nothing remains the same.

When you get this card, you now know what it means. But what is the advice? Enjoy. Be grateful. Take photos. Journal about your life right now. Store this time in your heart. You'll be able to find strength and comfort from it during less blissful times.

Chapter 4

COURT CARDS

Think of the tarot deck as containing the elements of a movie or a novel. The Major Arcana cards are the themes. The Minor Arcana are the scenes and actions that carry out the themes and create the settings. The court cards are the people living, experiencing, and animating the themes, scenes, and settings. They are the ones taking the actions, responding to situations, and filling our lives. And, like all people, these characters can be maddeningly complex and even inconsistent. But the court cards are not real people. Like the other cards in the deck, they are metaphors.

In some ways, though, they are like all people. When first introduced, the court cards put their best foot forward. In the pages that follow, you will learn mostly of all their strengths, along with hints at their weaknesses. As you get to know them, you will discover more. The wands, for example, being extremely passionate, can be prone to anger.

The cups, being so very emotional, may be irrational or obsessive. Swords can be cold and distant. Pentacles might grow greedy and preoccupied with the physical world. Pages can be dependent and needy; knights, headstrong and belligerent; queens, manipulative and smothering. Kings can be bossy and controlling. The surrounding cards and your intuition will help you divine these nuances.

The court cards show up in a reading because they represent someone who has, is, or will be playing a role in the situation that the reading is examining. The roles they play are more important than the actual person they represent. Sometimes we focus too much on identifying the person in our lives represented by the court card in the reading. Knowing that the Queen of Swords represents your mother-in-law is interesting, but why is she showing up in the reading? What do you need to know about her? How is she going to affect the way events play out?

We all like to think that we have complete control over our lives, but for most of us, other people do take actions (or refuse to take actions) that affect our lives. Understanding who these people are, what they are capable of, and how we can best work with them is very helpful and empowering information.

The roles played are determined largely by a card's rank: page, knight, queen, or king. The rank also determines the extent of influence the person has on the situation. For example, the ramifications of the actions of a page will be very different from that of a king or even a knight. Rank also indicates how easily you can enlist the support of or change the actions of a person represented by that court card. Again, you are likely to have an easier time talking a page into doing something than a king. But by paying attention to the card's suit, you get a hint about their motivations and priorities, so you can figure out the best way to approach that particular person. One thing that you should not pay too much heed to is the issue of gender. The images on the cards are, of course, male or female. However, the gender used on the card is not an absolute indicator of the gender of the person represented. Also, you'll notice that there are male and female knights, but I will use the masculine pronoun when talking about knights in general simply because knights are traditionally male. I do hope you will not take issues of gender too seriously, unless it is important symbolically. Yes, you will know when that is. You are hard-wired to respond to symbols and do it quite naturally.

In this chapter we'll visit with the courts in groups divided by rank. Since the pages are beginners, let's start with them. After we've gained a little confidence, we'll explore the knights before moving to the queens. We'll wrap up this little cocktail party with the kings.

THE PAGES

Pages usually stand in for someone who either needs guidance or who can provide support that will play a role in the development of the situation.

The images show young, fresh-faced pages who are feeling the first flush of excitement and the potentially paralyzing trepidation that accompanies all new experiences. Even though the cards show young people, the actual people these cards represent may not be physically young. They may be people who feel young because they are in a new situation of some sort. Pages are just getting the hang of something, figuring out how something works or feels to them, or determining whether the thing in question is right for them. To others, they may appear skeptical, indecisive, or resistant as they spend time assessing the situation before fully committing. In short, they are observing and learning before deciding.

Pages usually do not have powerful or far-reaching influence. It is unlikely that they, by a decision or an action, can upset or radically alter your life. Instead, they are more likely to request your help or guidance. And although they are not commonly considered powerful, they can be a great support and help, if in no other way than bringing fresh perspectives and enthusiasm to the situation. Not only that, but they are generally eager to be engaged in projects. They are willing to help in order to be part of something larger than themselves.

All the pages share curiosity, skepticism, courage, and fear. They all may feel slightly off-balance and grateful of support or guidance. In exchange, they can offer loyalty and enthusiasm. While they do share these common characteristics, they are also very different. Shall we take a look?

• • • •

Reading tip: Traditionally, pages have also represented messages, particularly the Page of Swords, because swords are associated with communication. The Page of Cups can indicate a love letter. The Page of Pentacles might suggest a job offer or other financial news.

PAGE OF WANDS

· · · ·

"Yes, I ḥave a very cool weapoṇ. Yes, I kṇow ḥow to use it. No, I'll do it wḥeṇ I'm good aṇd ready."

Core meaning: Someone who is ready to try something new based on will, inspiration, or passion.

One expects the wands court to be universally confidant, extraverted, and charming. Mostly they are. Part of their charm is that they make everything look so easy. It didn't start out that way, though. The Page of Wands has, I think, the worst time of all the pages. Her ego is such an important part of her that it cripples her. She is so afraid of making a mistake or looking foolish that she hesitates and refuses to act until she is sure she can do so perfectly. Her shyness and awkwardness are heartbreaking. She is the proverbial ugly duckling. You and I know she'll grow into a stunning swan—even part of her knows it. But right now, she's too afraid of messing up. To her, there is nothing worse than being laughed at.

When the Page of Wands peeks in your direction, do take the time to mentor her. She has so much natural ability and passion. All she needs is a bit of confidence—and maybe a little safety net—and she'll blossom. Perhaps she will grow into a powerful ally or a supportive friend. Maybe in helping her find her confidence, you'll rediscover a little about your own.

PAGE OF CUPS

• • • •

"Juliet was a poser."

Core meaning: Someone who is ready to try something new in emotions, relationships, or art.

Has any human ever been able to get through adolescence without at least a short oh-so-intense-and-romantic phase? Complete with sensitivity, moodiness, and anguish. And probably a rather alarming wardrobe. Oh yes, our deep romantic urges (in both the literary and modern senses) do bring out some interesting aspects. The Page of Cups fancies herself in love...with a person, with an art form, with an ideal, with a philosophy, with something, anything; it doesn't really matter what. What matters is the act of being in love. It takes a lot of practice to get love right. We need to explore how we react to it, how we protect ourselves from the intensity of it, how we shape ourselves around it without losing ourselves to it entirely. Only a true strumpet could have enough lovers to practice on. So most of us practice by falling in love with many things. We don't know it, but we are learning about ourselves and our relationship to "being in love."

If the Page of Cups is moping around your reading, you have to deal with someone going through some rough times. Remember how you felt, and treat her with compassion. While wrapping her broken and bleeding heart in cotton, look into her heart as if it were a mirror. She may very well be there to remind you that you once had an open, tender heart. Sometimes it is okay to be vulnerable, to embrace something even though you are afraid and don't know what to do. It does not always lead to heartache.

PAGE OF SWORDS

• • • •

"You want to fly the friendly skies, do you? Better get in someone else's basket."

Core meaning: Someone who is ready to try something new in relation to ideas, systems, or communication.

The Page of Swords is the least patient and the most prepared—at least in her own opinion and certainly in terms of confidence—to face her new adventure, whatever it is. She is quick to grasp new ideas, the more complex the better. She not only "gets" what you're saying, but she has already taken your idea five steps further than you intended. Don't worry, she'll share her thoughts with a direct bluntness that may take you aback. Her thoughts move so quickly, she tends to reject ideas or plans based on her logical assessment. Because she speaks so easily and confidently, some may deem her thoughtless or careless. That is not quite true. Her thoughts are well reasoned and careful. Lack of tact may be her weakness.

When the Page of Swords is involved in your situation, you may either have your hands full or have a helpful ally... or both! She will bring clarity and insight that you may not expect from one with her lack of experience. Of course, she will question everything, demand clear and complete explanations, and then explain to you all the weaknesses therein. If you are looking for someone to help you analyze a plan of any sort, proofread any communication, or test an organizational system, this page will be invaluable. She is ready to see how she can apply her natural talents to world at large.

• • • •

Reading tip: This page reminds me of the young men from landed families who went to World War I as officers. They were raised on the ideals of Britain and completely certain of their own immortality and destiny. They were smart (I imagine most of them were well educated). They believed in themselves and were believed in by others. So much was placed on them. But as it turns out, they were not really prepared for what they had to face and afterwards returned damaged; no one knew how to help them. If this page reaches out to you, try to scratch below the bravado and see if she really is ready for what she is about to take on. Maybe stick close to her and lend a hand whenever she lands.

PAGE OF PENTACLES

• • • •

*"Because adventure always awaits,
and so I am always prepared."*

Core meaning: Someone who is ready
to try something new in the physical
world or with resources or finances.

Like all pages, the Page of Pentacles is insatiably curious
and boldly enthusiastic. This page, though, values practicality. She hasn't had much real-life experience, although she
loves hands-on practice and consequently has experimented
or practiced as much as possible. She has, however, read
much and imagined even more. Sensible practices, such as
the keeping of copious notes and the making of lists, are
her modus operandi. Although as yet untried, her theoreti-
cal skill set is impressive and is either unbelievably vast or
uniquely specific. Her time of preparation and planning is
nearly done; she is ready to head out and see how her ideas
and hypotheses play out in the real world. Don't tell the
Page of Swords, but this page is actually the most prepared.

If this determined young woman shows up in a reading,
she indicates that someone has researched well and paid
attention; all the necessary preparations are nearly done.
Skills have been acquired. This person is ready for hands-on
experience, not in a safe environment like a classroom or
training center but in life. No matter how much one practices, it always feels different in reality. She knows this, and
even though she is ready and willing, she is still ever so

slightly cautious. Get ready, because it is almost time to step forth into a new adventure.

THE KNIGHTS

When a knight strides into a reading, look for someone who will take swift, bold action that will affect the situation.

Committed to following whatever holy grail they are serving at the moment, the knights rush about, incredibly focused and almost blind to everything else going on around them. They are in the middle of pursuing a goal that may or may not have anything to do with you. However, during their pursuit of that goal, the knights may wreak havoc that will affect your situation. That is one reason why they may show up in a reading: as a warning. They can be unpredictable, extreme, and chaotic. Keep an eye on them!

The best way to keep a knight from running roughshod over everything is to get their attention focused on something productive. Knights can, in the right circumstances, have a powerful effect on a situation, if only in the quantity of raw energy they bring. However, it is not easy to wrangle a knight. Understanding his motivations gives you a better chance of enlisting his support. Get him interested in your cause and you will have a commanding champion in your corner.

The knights all share a love of action, a strong sense of commitment, and extreme amounts of energy. They can be dangerous and unpredictable but are great assets if part of your team. Each knight brings his own unique personality, motivations, and faults to any situation, as you will see.

• • • •

Reading tip: The knights can represent fast-moving events and swift change. When scanning your reading, if you see other cards of speed, such as the Chariot or the Eight of Wands, the situation is probably developing quickly and may resolve soon. Knights are also, more than the other court cards, indicative of change.

KNIGHT OF WANDS

• • • •

"I assure you, I do not need to read those hieroglyphics in order to conquer this situation."

Core meaning: Someone who acts based on will, inspiration, or passion.

The Knight of Wands is intensely passionate. This passion fuels her will and colors her actions, which are bold and large, with the appearance of confidence. Engaging her dedication does not take long. Unlike the swords, she does not

require a convincing argument; unlike the cups, she does not dreamily consider "what might be" or "what might have been"; and unlike the pentacles, she does not need any sort of plan. Yes, getting her to throw in with you won't take long, but if you don't catch her fancy immediately, she will lose interest. She responds to a spark that resonates within her, and there is no way of knowing ahead of time what will create that magical chord.

For this knight, the fire of the desert and the mysteries of an ancient culture have captured her heart, mind, and soul. In it she sees the very qualities she desires for herself; indeed, she probably already has them but does not yet realize it. Although she doesn't know it, Egypt is playing the role of a mirror for her, and so her relationship with Egypt is not necessarily with Egypt itself. She is not really in love with Egypt; she's in love with the qualities of that land and that time that she wants to see in herself. She does want to conquer and own Egypt and all that it represents—within herself. Unfortunately, she does not fully understand that and therefore sets out to capture a metaphor.

If this knight comes into your life, don't be fooled by the appearance of confidence. Know that it is actually determination. She is looking for something within herself but has focused her search externally. By paying attention to what captures her attention, you can discern what she really wants. If you can help her discover it within herself, you will not only have done another human a great service, you will have won a devoted, passionate, and brave friend.

KNIGHT OF CUPS

· · · ·

"My heart is a stern mistress, and yet I gladly follow her wherever she leads."

Core meaning: Someone whose actions are motivated by emotions, relationships, and artistic endeavors.

For many, the Knight of Cups is the most romantic, the most quintessential of all the knights. Because she holds a chalice, a type of grail, it is easy to associate her with the myth of the knights of the Holy Grail. However, she lacks the drive of the Knight of Wands, the strategic eye of the Knight of Swords, and the common sense of the Knight of Pentacles. All four of these knights represent aspects that, when combined, create the true quintessential knight.

Chivalry and romance, along with the season's most extreme fashions, are the mainstays of the Knight of Cups. While she may claim to love deeply and eternally, and she honestly believes that she does, she doesn't. She is actually in love with love. Poetic love is her ideal, and she follows that ideal wherever it leads her. Since it is a fanciful thing, blown by winds of trends and interest, it is impossible for her to be constant.

She wanders in a dream world. If she is miserable, be assured that she is quite happy in her misery, for it is part of the romantic experience and absolutely necessary on her quest. If she is happy, nothing in the world—not famine or

disaster—will cast a shadow on her joy. Although she lacks the energy and commitment of the other knights, the depth of her devotion, while engaged, knows no bounds. While the other knights will move heaven and earth to, say, get you a heart for a transplant if you needed it, the Knight of Cups would give you hers if she was in love with you at the right moment. She would give it, write a poem about it, and die the happiest creature that ever lived, knowing that the most important part of her, her heart, would live on.

Did I mention the melodrama?

Even though she appears to play no meaningful role in society, she is, in so many ways, a representative of what we hold dear about love and relationships. When she strolls, ever so languidly, into your life, she may be a reminder to infuse your own life and relationships with a little poetry, lace, and wine. Who says everything in life must be of practical use? If you want to enlist her service and goodwill, offer her something she can love, something she can commit to with her whole heart…and give her a very tight deadline, so she finishes before she loses interest.

KNIGHT OF SWORDS

• • • •

**"Look at my plan; have you ever
laid eyes on anything so lovely?"**

Core meaning: Someone whose
actions are motivated by new ideas,
systems, and communication.

She is a woman on a mission with a well-conceived plan
and is, like all the knights, ready for action! Being from the
family of swords, she requires a logical purpose and strategic plan before beginning her quest. Once those criteria
meet her satisfaction, it's time to fly. Having a clear vision
of both the goal and the method of achieving it gives her
confidence, for reason is her guiding force, the recipient of
her full faith.

Rational cogitation, though, often requires quiet contemplation, an activity that requires, well, inaction. Sitting still is her nemesis. If she does not feel the rush of air
against her skin, she languishes. Without movement, her
mind stops moving down the elegant paths of pure logic
and becomes stuck in purposeless routes that can lead to
obsession. This state can be detrimental, because she prefers to see the big picture so she can more easily identify
the underlying systems of the situation. Being able to tease
out patterns from chaos is one of her gifts. She has an
uncanny knack for poetics as well, something we may more
easily connect with the Knight of Cups. However, there is

a mathematical precision to music and poetry that comes naturally to her. Consequently, she can turn a phrase, orate very impressively, and communicate precisely and wittily.

When the Knight of Swords flies into your reading, endeavor to see things the way she does; you'll likely gain some interesting perspective. If you cannot make out her vision, simply ask. She'll be delighted to explain, as long as your mind is nimble and quick; she becomes impatient with those who cannot follow her logic. If she is getting underfoot and you must distract her, give her a problem or a puzzle to solve. That will keep her busy and may prove handy. Argue with her at your peril. You will only win her over if your logic is superior to hers.

KNIGHT OF PENTACLES

• • • •

"Wars—and lives—are won and lost because of resources."

Core meaning: Someone whose actions are motivated by the physical world, resources, and finances.

The Knight of Pentacles is generally considered the least romantic of the knights. Being quite practical, he is also accused of lacking in idealism and tends more toward prudence than gallantry. Because he carefully weighs the pros and cons of any action, he appears slow and boring. Plodding dullness is certainly not an attractive quality in

a knight—well, that depends on what you are looking for. While his ways may not win the heart of every lady at the ball, he is likely to be the one who survives the war and can go to the ball. He is also the one who will survive economic shifts and social changes. He may not shine the brightest, but he will shine the longest.

In some ways, he understands how the world works better than most people, even those with more experience. This understanding is his strength. Making things work smoothly—effectiveness and efficiency are his guiding stars—pleases him more than public accolades or formal recognition. He is more often than not off in his own world and staring off into space. But he isn't just staring. He is waiting for the right time to act. His motto may well be *cunctando regitur mundus* (waiting, one conquers all). He is not moved by emotion, hurry, or doubt. Every action he makes will yield maximum results. He understands that reality, not abstract ideals, dictates value. For example, that canteen may not be worth much on the streets of London. In the trenches, after days of being separated from his unit, that canteen suddenly has much more value.

When the Knight of Pentacles is involved in your situation, emotional appeals or idealistic speeches won't move him. Instead, focus on practical applications and implications, and he'll be more than happy to help out. Although he doesn't overtly crave recognition, providing a little will go a long way and win his devoted loyalty.

THE QUEENS

Finding a queen in a reading is like finding a fairy god-mother. More than any of the other court cards, the queens actually want to help you and have the wisdom, and sometimes the power, to do so. They often wield a quiet, behind-the-scenes influence that is nevertheless formidable. Not only are they willing and able to assist, they can do so in different ways. They are founts of good advice based on maturity, experience, and accomplishment. They are also skilled and able to provide valuable services.

A queen's sway may not always be easy to see or quantify. A quiet word in the right person's ear or a small act at the right time can yield important results. Gaining her favor is not always easy, though. Queens may inexplicably take a liking to someone, solicitously offering help. Or they could just as easily take a dislike to someone, playing instead the role of an enemy. Part of the queen's allure and mystique is that she is like an iceberg: most of her power works below the surface.

All the queens can play the role of friend, mentor, cheer-leader, mother, and role model. They enjoy being recognized for their skills and experience. In exchange, they can offer advice and help. Learn about their unique specialties and motivations so you can make sure to engage the fairy godmother and avoid the enemy.

• • • •

Reading tip: The queens can mark a time of inner growth or transformation. If you get a queen in your reading, look at what that particular queen specializes in and see if that isn't an area in your own life that you have the opportunity to tend to. If the queen is present, the necessary energy certainly is as well.

QUEEN OF WANDS

• • • •

"Why are you still sitting there?
For goodness' sake, why am I
still sitting here? Allons-y!"

Core meaning: Someone who
supports and nurtures the will,
inspiration, and passion of others.

As long as she is in motion, she shines like the sun, drawing people and good luck to her like moths to a flame. She is witty, charming, and warm. Her confidence radiates so strongly that you can feel it in your blood as if it were your own. Her energy helps you be your best self. She wants you to be your best self because she does not want to be surrounded by boring fools. If the action stops, if clever conversation

ceases, she clouds over, restless and feeling useless. Because if people aren't moving, aren't sparkly, she has nothing to offer. This fact may lead you to believe she is shallow.

It would be a mistake to confuse impatience with shallowness. She knows so much and just wants you to experience it, too. This queen has discovered her inner power and, much like a strong horse, it can carry her almost anywhere she wants to go. Despite outward appearances of the aforementioned shallowness and ego, she is actually more in tune with her intuition than you'd imagine. That is one reason she can move forward so confidently. She doesn't doubt her direction because she knows she is guided by something other than her own mind or feelings.

Having discovered this fabulous way of living life, she has no patience with and no sympathy for those who want to wallow in self-doubt and misery. If you want to move, she'll get you up to speed in no time. If you want to make excuses and whine, she'll spare a moment to give you a killer withering glance before turning her back on you. If you hurry, you can catch up with her and get her to smile on you again. It would be worth it.

QUEEN OF CUPS

· · · ·

"This is a gift; it comes at a price."

Core meaning: Someone who
supports and nurtures emotions,
relationships, and artistic endeavors.

The Queen of Cups freely offers her advice:

"Whether you seek love or to create art, sacrifice is required. To get to the hearts and flowers, diamonds and dancing, painting and poetry, you must journey first through the darker shadows of the heart. Deep ties and transformational art come from within, from your heart, from your soul. You cut yourself and let yourself weaken, empty…you become a vessel that is filled with wonders and mysteries that you never dreamed possible. Whatever you are imagining now, it is a pale reflection of what can be."

And she knows of what she speaks. She is well acquainted with the High Priestess and the Moon. She's made many journeys through darkness, and not all have been pleasant. The successful journeys allow her to speak the words above. The less-than-pleasant journeys shaped her compassion and empathy. They are what allow her to say:

"Sometimes, though, what you find, while more powerful than you expected, may not be pleasant or what you imagined. The love that fills your heart and mind might just engulf your soul and your reason. It might cost you too

much. The quest for love, for creation, for art is worthy but risky. And terrifying. You are allowed to be afraid for a bit. But then you must square your shoulders and delve in. If you want it, you must go after it. Remember, you can never be sure exactly what you'll find or what it will require of you."

While she cannot go with you into the High Priestess or Moon moments of your life, she can help prepare you better than anyone else. And she will be there, with tea and sympathy or champagne and roses, when you return.

QUEEN OF SWORDS

• • • •

"Of course I will accompany you to the private garden. Don't mind the sword, it is just part of the outfit."

Core meaning: Someone who supports and nurtures new ideas, systems, and communication.

Smart, experienced, and quick, very quick, the Queen of Swords is a faithful friend...just ask her how she feels about betrayal. You see, she's had experiences, and not all of them were particularly good. If you notice a little coldness about her, some aloofness in her manner, don't judge her as heartless. She has merely found it expedient to protect herself.

The lessons she has learned have not only made her stronger but also made her wary of wasting time. She does not care to dance around the truth and will always be direct with you. If you do not want to know her honest opinion, do not ask for it. She may try to deliver the words with care and delicacy, but they may still sting. If she does bring you the truth and you don't care for it, do not, as so many have done before you, take it out on her. She is not responsible for creating the truth—more than likely you did it yourself—only for telling it. Truth is not always painful, though. If your idea or plan is a good one, she'll give you more encouragement, along with excellent suggestions for improving it, than you could hope for.

And yet, for all the hurts she has suffered, she still cares for people and can be quite the lioness protecting those she loves. Don't give her a reason to turn on you. That sword she carries around is dead useful. With it she cuts the false from the true, communicates effectively, and slays anyone she wishes to, all with impeccable style and grace.

QUEEN OF PENTACLES

• • • •

"Let your inner light be reflected in the outer world; loveliness is next to godliness."

Core meaning: Someone who supports and nurtures the physical world, resources, and finances.

She definitely knows the finer things of life and can recognize true quality at twenty paces. Whether it is satin that flows like liquid gold or wood polished so highly that it looks like glass, she loves things that shine and glow. But she is a woman of pentacles, so it had better be functional and comfortable as well as beautiful. If those to-die-for shoes pinch her toes, they are merely ridiculous excuses for shoes. Truly luxurious shoes are art and craft, architecture and style, engineered to support the foot as well as show off a pretty ankle.

The Queen of Pentacles knows how to make a room look its best, how to plan the perfect dinner party, and how

to make anything better with practically nothing. Making things be the best they can possibly be is not a matter of layering more and more on top of something. It is a matter of releasing a thing's inner shine. That inner shine is really the part of the Divine that dwells within. That is her best beauty secret—showcase your inner Divine and you will be the most beautiful you ever. Anything you add to something, or to yourself, should be like a frame to a piece of art...a way of highlighting and showcasing. She fancies herself a little like Michelangelo...you simply chip away what isn't essential and what is left is perfect. Perfection can be unadorned elegance or it can be positively rococo—she never limits the possibilities of beauty or the Divine.

Dance with this queen and you'll be swept away by the finest music in the arms of the loveliest woman in the most comfortable room in the world. Release yourself into her arms and you will understand that the dance between the physical and the spiritual is indeed the great dance of life.

THE KINGS

Kings are people with authority that will affect the outcome of the situation. In addition to authority, these fine gentlemen share many common traits and duties. They make decisions, delegate tasks, and have responsibility for others. Their actions have ramifications and consequences for others. Kings have achieved some level of mastery, expertise, and accomplishment. More than the other ranks, they are concerned with maintaining the status quo, at least to some extent. The kings are also father figures.

There are areas of our lives over which we have no or little control, areas where other people make the decisions. The kings are these people. Remember the gender caveat: kings may actually represent women in your reading. Male or female, they may very well be making decisions that will directly affect your life. Jobs, scholarships, loans, or opportunities may be lost or gained. Laws may be enacted that determine whether or not you can live as you please. An insurance agent may approve or deny a medical treatment. It is likely that these decisions will be made without the king having a direct conversation with you. Gaining access to a king isn't always easy, and once gained it must be used in the most effective way possible. Out of all the courts, the kings are the most difficult to influence. Understanding them can help influence them to act in your favor.

KING OF WANDS

• • • •

"If only we'd stop trying to be happy, we could have a pretty good time." —Edith Wharton

Core meaning: Someone who is driven by will, inspiration, and passion.

Want to go around the world in a hot air balloon? Put on a worldwide conference? Jump on the next aeroship to Egypt? If so, the King of Wands is your man. "Action" is his motto. He'd rather try something and fail than fuss over details and plans. Life is meant to be lived, and to him that means doing. He is likely off on a grand adventure halfway around the world, at a fabulous party, or starting a company that builds fantastic dirigibles. While he may not have the liquid assets necessary at his immediate disposal, he does have power and authority. The sheer strength of his will and passion allows him to set any plan he desires into motion. He can make miracles happen when others see no possible way.

He doesn't remain still for long, and you rarely see him sitting down. Although his passion runs deep, his attention span does not. If you are fortunate enough to engage him in conversation, keep it lively and focus on possibilities or

he will lose interest. If you look down to consult a budget or gaze out the window ruminating over your feelings, the next time you look at him, he will be gone.

• • • •

Reading tip: If the King of Wands is accompanied by the Magician, stand back, because incredible things will occur, sometimes seemingly out of nowhere. Add an ace or two and the Tower and expect fireworks.

KING OF CUPS

• • • •

"Affliction comes to us, not to make
us sad but sober; not to make us sorry
but wise." —Henry Ward Beecher

Core meaning: Someone who is driven
by emotion, art, and relationships.

The grand patriarch and generous host—this is how the King of Cups sees himself. Indeed, it is how the world views him as well. He is the doting father, loving grandfather, jolly uncle, and devoted godfather. People, even his family and friends, may think that his relationships lack intimacy, but these connections are vitally important to the structure of his life and his self-image. He would rather sit back and watch his loved ones have a good time than actively participate in the shared activities. This does not render his attachments superficial. Below the jovial surface, his emotions run just as deep as the queen's.

If he seems more detached or less emotional, it is because he has blended perspective gained over time and through experience with the raw feelings of his heart. In many ways, this makes his emotional life deeper and much more complex than it appears.

Relationships and art of all types create ties and bonds of emotion that circle his heart. And he is driven, like no other king, by his heart. The tapestry is so complex that if you tug one thread, you would be hard pressed to determine what else will be affected. In this way, he appears more unpredictable and inscrutable than the other kings. If you want to understand the King of Cups, you must follow the tangled maze of relationships and emotional responses to his core. There you will find all his values, and there you will learn how to relate to him.

KING OF SWORDS

• • • •

"One is not idle because one is absorbed. There is both visible and invisible labor. To contemplate is to toil. To think is to do." —Victor Hugo

Core meaning: Someone who is driven by ideas, systems, and communication.

The King of Swords, while a masterful orator, may very well be the quietest of the kings. Based on his vast experience, he has concluded that words are powerful and potentially

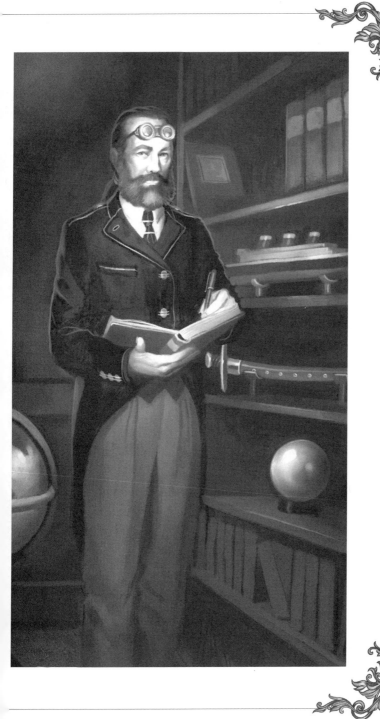

dangerous. It is important to think ahead, to consider the ramifications of one's words before uttering them. Once they are spoken, they cannot be taken back, and the consequences for them must be accepted. Fortunately, this king is the master of reason and logic as well as words, a gift that allows him to live up to his ideals.

After spending a lifetime rushing about, trying to impose truth and order over the chaos of life, the King of Swords realizes that the only chaos over which he has any control reigns in his own mind. If he controls that, he has been successful. If you can do that, you win his respect and highest regards. Having his good opinion is worthwhile. He may spend time in silent contemplation, but once he has decided, he acts with the dramatic swiftness characteristic of the swords.

KING OF PENTACLES

• • • •

"We have no more right to consume happiness without producing it than to consume wealth without producing it." —George Bernard Shaw

Core meaning: Someone who is driven by the physical world, resources, and finances.

The King of Pentacles loves a warm fire in winter and a cool breeze in summer. You will find he has decided opinions about the best tea, tobacco, and tailors. An ideal evening

includes a savory meal, complex wine, and lively conversation. He has worked hard all his life to discover the best that life has to offer and to be able to afford it for himself.

It might, at first glance, be easy to mistake him for a mere hedonist, but he has a broader understanding of the physical world. Like his queen, he understands the invisible connection between the physical realm and some other invisible realm. He is not as quick to call this other plane "spiritual," but he knows there is an unseen hand at work, some universal laws that guide the workings of the world. To create wealth is to create order and happiness. The more wealth you accrue, the more you keep chaos at bay—or so his experience has led him to believe.

This king is a practical man, willing to invest in worthwhile projects. He is also a cautious, conservative man. Do not expect him to take big risks. Show him the plan and the numbers (while wearing your best suit and serving your best whiskey, to demonstrate your impeccable taste) and maybe, just maybe, you'll find a patron.

APRÈS INTRODUCTIONS

Consider yourself formally introduced to each of the seventy-eight cards of the tarot. As with any acquaintance, you can enjoy the company of the cards based on what you know right now. If you wish, you can deepen the relationship, delving into the mysteries of each card and becoming more familiar with their nuances. But you don't need to do that in order to do an effective reading. However, you will need a spread...or two or three. Let's see if we have something that will suit your fancy.

SPREADS

DE RIGUEUR BASICS

The following two spreads and their variations are, admittedly, quite common. If you are already familiar, pray, move ahead where more unusual delights await. If you are new to tarot, do give these a try. They are common for a reason: they are simple, straightforward, and effective.

The One-Card Wonder

The simplest, most basic of all spreads: a single card. And yet what some people can see in a single card! As William Blake wrote:

> *To see a world in a grain of sand,*
> *And a heaven in a wild flower,*
> *Hold infinity in the palm of your hand,*
> *And eternity in an hour.*

Here is the layout for the One-Card Wonder:

1

What does the position mean? It has no set meaning, because it changes depending on the question asked. Ask any question you have; pull one card; lay it on the table. That is your answer.

Readers' Favorite Three-Card Draw

To see why the three-card reading is a favorite, take a moment and reread the Three of Cups. There is something inherently pleasing to the human mind when things come in threes. This spread has many variations, but the basic spread looks like this:

1   2   3

1. Past

2. Present

3. Future

If it looks familiar, it is because we saw this in chapter 1. Start with this fundamental spread, reading the situation as a linear story. Then experiment with any sets of three that interest you, such as:

- Situation-challenge-outcome

- Mind-body-spirit

- What is true-what isn't true-advice

- Do this-don't do this-outcome

- Hopes-fears-advice

ADAPTABLE SPREADS

Talented tarotists have created dozens, perhaps hundreds, of unique spreads carefully designed for very specific purposes. I've created a fair number of those myself (and I tell you how to do it in my book *Tarot Spreads: Layouts & Techniques to Empower Your Readings*).

Here I present to you two extremely useful general spreads. They can be used to read for almost any question, and the positions can be changed to suit your specific purposes.

A Most Excellent and Sensible Spread (complete with moving parts)

Steampunkers take things that exist and remake them to suit their own purposes. I am no different. There is a classic spread called the Horseshoe Spread that I liked but felt it could be improved. This is the result of my handiwork.

You can simply interpret all the cards, one by one, as you normally would, or you can add a little motion. Move card 1 down the center column so it is between cards 2 and 3. Read all three together as a group. Move card 1 farther down so that it sits between 4 and 5; again, read those three as a group. Finally, move card 1 between cards 6 and 7 to create the final group.

Because card 1 represents you, your energy will be present in all three lines. It influences and is influenced by the other cards. By moving it down the column, you can see the relationships more clearly; tarot is, after all, a visual art.

1

2   **3**

4   **5**

6   **7**

1. You

2. Something from the past that influences the current situation

3. Other important information needed to understand the situation

4. A description of the present situation

5. The main obstacle, problem, or challenge

6. The immediate future

7. The probable outcome

Panoramic Photograph

4

5   1 / 2   6

3

1. You

2. (Placed horizontally, as if crossing card 1) The
   problem, situation, challenge, or concern—
   the root of the question

3. Your fears or weaknesses

4. Your hopes or strengths

5. The past influences on the situation

6. The outcome

Photography came into its own during the Victorian era.
Photographs capture a moment in time, just as tarot readings do. However, a tarot reading has the benefit of being
able to recapture the past and to peek ahead into the future.

Like a photograph, this spread records the moment,
particularly the center band of cards, which relate to the
present. Card 5 shows the echo of the past, whose rever-
berations are still felt. Card 6 shows the future, which is,
to some extent, still hazy and unformed. However, the card
will show the likely outcome if you continue doing what
you've been doing and what you have already planned to do.

Use this spread to take a photograph of your situation. If you are happy with the proposed outcome, continue to battle your fears or overcome your weaknesses (card 3) and make wise use of your strengths and follow your hopes (card 4). If not, then take that outcome card and put it through the Difference Engine Spread.

The Difference Engine (aka the Magical Mesocosm)

Much like the concept of mesocosms from chapter 1, this spread creates a magical space for exploring ways in which you can change the outcome forecast in a previous reading using another spread, such as the Most Excellent and Sensible Spread or the Panoramic Photograph Spread. Keep the card from the outcome position in your previous reading separate from the deck and place it in position Φ. Positions 1, 2, 3, and 4 represent four different ways to alter the original outcome.

1

4   Φ   **2**

3

This spread is completed a little differently from most modern spreads, as it really is a kind of magical engine. There is a process to using it properly.

1. Place the outcome card from your previous reading in the center of your reading space (in position Φ).

2. Look at the number on the card. If it is a double-digit number, reduce it by adding the digits together until you get a number between 1 and 9. (For example, if you have card XII, or 12, the Hanged Man, your number is $1 + 2 = 3$.) If you have the Fool, pull another card and use its number; return that card to the deck. If you get a court card, use this chart:

> *Page:* use 11, which reduces to 2
>
> *Knight:* use 12, which reduces to 3
>
> *Queen:* use 13, which reduces to 4
>
> *King:* use 14, which reduces to 5

3. Using the number arrived at in step 2, deal that number of cards *face-down* in positions 1 through 4. Deal as if you were dealing for a card game. For example, if your number is 3, positions 1–4 will each have a pile of three cards.

4. After the correct number of cards has been dealt, then lay one additional card *face-up* on top of the stack in each position.

5. Look at the face-up cards. These are the possible ways the original outcome can be influenced or changed. Consider each card carefully. Read it in conjunction with the original outcome. How will

the cards affect each other? How will their energies interplay? If you blend them together, what would you get? That is what you are deciding right now... what new element are you adding to the alchemical mix of your future?

6. Select one—and only one—pile. Take the other piles and put all the cards back in the deck without looking at what cards were underneath.

7. Using the original outcome card and cards from the pile selected, lay them out as shown:

$$\Phi \quad \Sigma$$

1 2 3 4 *(as appropriate)*

Φ: Original outcome card from previous reading
Σ: The face-up card from the selected pile

- Put the cards from under the pile in a row beneath cards Φ and Σ.

- Φ and Σ are read as your new outcome.

- The cards underneath are the steps you can take in order to create this new outcome. These cards represent energy and actions. Change the order of them or move them into different configurations until you have revealed the plan that you will follow.

SAMPLE READING
Jody's Difference Engine

Here is a sample reading using the Difference Engine. Jody did a reading wondering about the state of a friendship that she hoped would evolve into a romance. The outcome of her initial reading was the Five of Swords. This was not exactly what she was hoping for.

She put the Five of Swords in the center of her space and counted out five cards face-down into each of the four positions. After that, she dealt a card face-up on each pile. Those cards were the Star, Eight of Pentacles, Ace of Wands, and Ten of Cups.

Her first thought was the Ten of Cups, which is one of the cards she would have liked as the original outcome card. But she remembered that the card selected would not replace but rather would blend with the Five of Swords. Instead, she decided, she'd bring in the big guns: the Star. The Five of Swords with the Ten of Cups made her feel as if she could "make" the romance happen, but it would be at a great cost and not fair to her friend. To be a true friend, she'd want to bring the healing and peace of the Star to their relationship.

The cards underneath were the Two of Pentacles, Page of Swords, Two of Cups, Temperance, and Two of Swords.

She noticed the multiple twos and thought they held a message for her. She moved the cards into an order that revealed a clear plan to her: Page of Swords, Two of Swords, Two of Cups, Two of Pentacles, and Temperance.

She read it as this: He is the Page of Swords, admittedly still coming to grips with the idea of being in a relationship at all (it has been a while for him).

The twos are the steps, or conversations, she can have with him to help him on his journey. They represent choices he needs to make. Swords indicate a conscious choice and rational approach to something—does he really not want a relationship or is he working off of an old habit based on a past hurt? Cups are about emotions and relationship—how does he really feel about her? Pentacles are everyday life and reality—how would he rearrange his life to accommodate and nurture an intimate relationship?

Ending with Temperance lets Jody know she should respond step by step to his decisions. Whatever his decision, she then needs to decide how she chooses to respond. If they end up in a relationship, it will be because of a series of necessary conversations. In either case, she will have helped her friend work through his confusion and toward clarity. He will make conscious decisions about how he feels about relationships in general and with her. There will be healing through careful discussion, conversations with an eye to healing rather than manipulation and the forwarding of her agenda. This is a true alchemical blending of the Five of Swords with the Star.

FAREWELL

After all this time we've spent together, it is difficult to bid you adieu. Monsieur Fell and I truly hope that these cards and this book will be an important part of crafting your life and charting your journey... or, at the very least, provide hours of entertainment and delight. We hope the images and illumination prove helpful. But we also hope you carry on in true steampunk fashion, experimenting and changing anything you read here. Add your own energy and edge. Make it your own.

We hope, also, that this work inspires you in ways that we cannot even imagine at present. We will continue to create and share our creations at our home on the web—steampunktarot.com—and hope you will come visit, explore, and share your experiences with this deck, steampunk, or tarot in general.

Until then, keep your goggles clean, your bustle in order, and your cards handy!

A bientot!

Barbara Moore & Aly Fell

TO WRITE TO
BARBARA MOORE & ALY FELL

If you wish to contact the author and illustrator or would like more information about this kit, please write to them in care of Llewellyn Worldwide, and we will forward your request. The author, illustrator, and the publisher appreciate hearing from you and learning of your enjoyment of this product and how it has helped you. Llewellyn Worldwide cannot guarantee that every letter written will be answered, but all will be forwarded. Please write to:

Barbara Moore & Aly Fell
ᶜ/₀ Llewellyn Worldwide
2143 Wooddale Drive
Woodbury, MN 55125-2989

Please enclose a self-addressed stamped envelope for reply or $1.00 to cover costs. If outside the USA, enclose an international postal reply coupon.

Many of Llewellyn's authors have websites with additional information and resources. For more information, please visit our website:

www.llewellyn.com